Salon Management

To my grandchildren – Lorraine, Jennifer, Michèle, Matthew, Jacqui, Michael, Joanna, Stephen.

Salon Management for Hairdressers and Beauty Therapists

T.W. Masters Dip.FE.,CGIA.

Gower Technical Press

Published by
Gower Technical Press Limited,
Gower House,
Croft Road,
Aldershot,
Hants GU11 3HR,
England.

Gower Publishing Company,
Old Post Road,
Brookfield,
Vermont 05036,
U.S.A.

Printed and bound in Great Britain by
Redwood Burn Limited, Trowbridge, Wiltshire

British Library Cataloguing in Publication Data

Masters, T. W.
  Salon management for hairdressers and
  beauty therapists.
  1. Beauty shops – Great Britain –
  Management   2. Hairdressing – Great Britain
  – Management
  I. Title
  646.7′2′068   TT965

Library of Congress Cataloging-in-Publication Data

Masters, T. W.
  Salon management for hairdressers and beauty
  therapists.

  Bibliography: p.
  1. Beauty shops – Management.   I. Title.
  TT965.M37   1987   646.7′26′068   87-11902

ISBN 0 291 39709 3

Contents

Preface

It is self-evident that the basic requirements of a hairdressing or beauty therapy business include suitable premises, effective equipment, technically skilled staff and adequate finance to operate, but there is one other equally essential ingredient which adds the final touch – *good management*.

There has to be more to the popular hairdressing or beauty therapy salon than the goods, chattels and practical skills of the trade. These are service industries which are labour-intensive and often involve personal relationships with the clients who visit the salon. Clients not only have rights, they also have expectations – ways in which they hope to be treated in terms of care, attention and ultimate satisfaction. While clients visit the salon primarily for a hairdressing service or a beauty treatment they also quite reasonably expect to enjoy the experience. Employees equally expect to perform their allotted tasks in a congenial workplace and to be suitably rewarded. The employer anticipates a satisfied clientele, a happy staff and not least a profitable return on an often quite substantial investment. When parties enter into a contract, whether it be as employer, employee or client they each expect there will be something in it for them as individuals.

In order to be successful a manager requires a wide ranging knowledge and sympathetic understanding of all relevant matters both material and aesthetic. Some of these things may come quite naturally to the lucky business but in most cases much thought and careful organization is required for complete or near complete success.

A recent nationwide survey published by the Joint Training Council for the Hairdressing Industry in conjunction with the Manpower Services Commission showed that among other things:

* nearly three-quarters of the hairdressing salons covered in the survey catered mainly for women, nearly one-quarter were unisex and only one in fourteen catered mainly for

men; (Readers will notice that I refer to clients as female throughout the book – most are, but I do not wish to imply any discrimination against their male counterparts. After all, hair grows as fast on men as on women!)

* few salons offered additional beauty treatments except perhaps manicure and the majority of those which did offer a full range of beauty treatments were among the larger salons;

* over three-quarters of the salons were independent as opposed to being part of a chain;

* the most common size of salon was three to five hairdressing staff including the manager;

* over three-quarters of managers owned the salons in which they worked;

* over three-quarters of the hairdressing staff were women and more than one-half of the managers were women;

* the majority of hairdressing staff tended to be young with only one in six aged 36 or over;

* the majority of managers were trained hairdressers and the small number who were not so trained were more likely to be managing larger salons.

A significant fact, probably self-evident to the keen observer, would seem to be that the vast majority of hairdressing salons are owned by private individuals trading on their own account in small to medium size salons. Moreover, while most of these working proprietors are trained hairdressers skilled in their craft *it is unlikely that very many of them will have received any formal training in the skills of business management* and depend largely upon their practical hairdressing ability to attract custom and generate revenue. To what extent their methods are cost-effective and how profitability relates to productivity may be quite another matter. Clearly the running of even the smallest salon must benefit from effective organization and if consistent growth is to occur knowledge and understanding of the principles of financial control and all supporting management skills is a necessity.

It is also apparent that very few of these salons offer additional beauty treatments. It would appear therefore that this potentially lucrative service is catered for mainly by a relatively small number of specialist beauty therapy salons with appropriately trained staff.

While parts of this book will tend to lean towards the present majority need, namely hairdressers, the text which follows sets out to cover management in the round supported by relevant aspects of finance and accounting, the law, the workforce, publicity and service to the clientele – all of which applies equally to hairdressing and beauty therapy businesses. It will therefore prove to be an invaluable reference work for potential and existing owners and managers as well as an indispensable study aid to those preparing for relevant examinations.

T.W. Masters

1
Setting up in business

Any hairdresser or beauty therapist contemplating going into business on their own account will, it is hoped, be suitably experienced in the technical and social requirements of that particular trade but it is unlikely that they will be equally well acquainted with the general and financial management skills so necessary for setting up and running a successful venture. Therefore it is essential to seek professional guidance on any aspect which is clearly outside day-to-day experience. The three most valuable potential allies will be a bank manager, an accountant, and a solicitor. The advice of the former may be relatively free but the latter two will certainly cost money, although future events may show this to be money well spent.

Running your own show means moving from a position of paid employment to self-employment and that has a number of quite significant implications. As a paid employee you will have been accustomed to working a set number of hours and being able to rely upon a wage packet or salary cheque at regular intervals with probably none of the direct responsibility of ensuring the money is there to provide the wages. Tax and insurance contributions will have been deducted at source and the net income earned will have been all yours to use for domestic and social purposes.

As a self-employed person or sole trader you will have to put in all the hours that the business demands and your income will be whatever the business can afford to allow you to draw. Never assume that the whole of the net profits are yours to do with as you will, *for always the business has first claim*. Profits will be taxed in their entirety under Schedule D and you will have to ensure that the appropriate portion is set aside to meet the annual tax bill. You will also have to buy your own National Insurance stamps, paying Class 2 and Class 4 contributions. If you employ staff you will need to find their wages out of revenue and cover all of the other costs of production and the overhead expenses of the business. It is as well to bear in mind that as a sole-trader you will be personally responsible for all of the debts of your business even to the extent of a claim on most of the goods and chattels of your own home in the event of failure.

Now let us take a more cheerful view and consider the satisfactions to be derived from being your own boss. If you have the right temperament, like responsibility, can handle difficult situations without getting flustered or losing your temper, are not afraid of hard work and inevitably longer hours than when you were in paid employment, can accept disappointments and still carry on smiling, have a well developed sense of where the real priorities lie and not least a fair sense of humour, then you could be moderately successful. Finally, while it is reasonable to assume that you will want to make satisfactory profits, if your sole objective in running your own business is simply to make lots and lots of money for yourself then in a personal service industry such as hairdressing or beauty therapy you may never know the pleasure to be gained from earning the confidence, respect and even affection of your clients.

Types of business

There are three ways in which the normal business may operate:

1 Sole trader

The sole trader, sometimes called the sole proprietor, is in fact a self-employed person. Sole trader does not mean that this is the only person working in the business. A sole trader business can support a considerable number of employees. The sole trader is entitled to all of the profits but is also personally responsible for all the liabilities, debts and losses to the extent that private possessions can be at the mercy of creditors in the event of the business failing. The sole trader makes all of the decisions and is free to choose how much money and time to put into the business and indeed how much money to take out. The sole trader has complete control over the day-to-day activities of the business and provided there is no breach of law is regularly answerable only to the Inland Revenue which is the official body with the power to question the accuracy of accounting with regard to returns in respect of taxes.

2 Partnership

A partnership is a venture in which two or more people pool financial resources, knowledge and expertise to jointly run a business. Like the sole trader a partnership can and often does employ other people who are not members of the partnership itself. A partnership falls into much the same category as a sole trader except that profits and liabilities are shared. The partners stand or fall financially together. The basis of every successful partnership must be one of understanding and complete trust, bearing in mind that each partner can enter into a contract on behalf of the partnership which becomes binding on all of the partners and that the creditors of an insolvent partner could put the whole partnership out of business. It is possible to put a limit on financial commitment by forming a limited partnership but at least one member must accept unlimited liability.

Limited partners cannot normally take an active part in management and have only limited rights. The limited partner is in effect little more than a financial backer for the business. Unlike the normal partnership a limited partnership must be registered with the appropriate official of the Department of Trade and Industry. Sleeping partners have the same unlimited responsibility for partnership debts as the general partners whether the partnership is limited or not. Sleeping partners can take part in the management of the business in an advisory capacity but generally their only involvement is in putting up some money in return for an agreed share of the profits. Although it is not strictly a legal requirement it is absolutely essential in the interests of all concerned to have a formal agreement drawn up which covers all of the points involved.

3 Private limited company

A private limited company can be formed with as few as two shareholders one of whom must be a director. A company secretary must be appointed who can be one of the shareholders or an outsider such as an accountant or a solicitor. Forming such a company puts the business under the protection which the law affords to a private limited company incorporated under the Companies Acts. When the business is incorporated it becomes a separate legal entity. Liabilities, debts and losses are then *entirely the company's responsibility*. The company is 'limited by shares' which means that the financial liability of the members of the company, the shareholders, is limited to the nominal value of the shares they hold.

The directors and the management are responsible to the company, the shareholders and the creditors but unlike the sole trader and ordinary partners who have unlimited liability for debts, they are liable only in specified circumstances.

Company law is too extensive and too complex to be explained in a book of this nature and anyone interested in trading as a legitimate company is advised to seek expert advice. It is sometimes considered that the formation of a company leads to ultimate success but for the most part corporate life is legally demanding and administration can prove to be expensive. The sole trader and the partnership lead a less complicated legal life and are generally free to choose their own route to success or failure. The main attraction of incorporation is to be personally set apart from financial liabilities, but limited liability can turn out to be something of an illusion with little real significance in a business that is financially successful.

Where personal service and the overt influence of the proprietor(s) is the essence of the business then it makes sense to operate as a sole trader or in a partnership. If on the other hand the personal touch is quite removed from customer relationships and it is advantageous to project a corporate image then a limited company may be the better vehicle. The personal financial protection of limited liability has its attractions but the precise nature of the business may well be the deciding factor. At least in the initial stages of developing a business which offers a very personal service such as hairdressing or beauty therapy there is much to be gained from close personal contact between the proprietor(s) and the clientele.

Premises

Premises can vary from ground floor street level to upper floors but unless there are adequate lift facilities anything above the first floor could prove to be inconvenient and certainly discouraging for older clients. Access can be difficult and even when there are suitable signs the premises could go largely unnoticed by casual passers by.

Street level premises will inevitably be more expensive in terms of rent and rates and in a prime position could cost more than the average small business could afford. Street level premises can be more difficult to keep clean and will probably be slightly more expensive to heat. Warm air rises and natural temperatures are lower at ground level. However they do have the advantage of a shop window or similar display area which can be a valuable means of advertising when used to maximum effect, with the additional benefit that it constitutes relatively cost-free publicity.

Taking over an existing business will obviously mean accepting the premises generally as they are and certainly where they are. The actual situation is a most important consideration. Alterations can be made to existing premises but there is no way they can be jacked-up and moved to another locality. Vacant premises pose much the same problem. Where it is apparent that the premises as they are will not meet long-term aims it is wise to assess their suitability for necessary alteration and to ensure that permission can be obtained for the work to be done.

Premises can be freehold or they can be leasehold. Clearly when the freehold is purchased the premises become the property of the trader once mortgage or loan commitments have been discharged and from then on there will be much greater freedom to make structural alterations. The most common basis for the occupation of business premises is leasehold and it is absolutely essential to ascertain what can or cannot be done under the terms and conditions of the lease.

Paying for it all

Unless you have inherited a large sum of money from a distant relative or had a win on the football pools there is probably only one way to acquire the necessary capital to start a business or buy an existing one – by borrowing.

Money is probably the most expensive thing you can buy and the lender will want, above all things, to be satisfied that the proposition is sound and the money lent reasonably secure. That is to say the revenue from the business can be expected to cover the interest charges and repay the principal in due time, and in the event of failure there will be adequate assets to cover the balance of the loan.

A bank is perhaps the most convenient source of finance for the small business but the bank manager will need to be convinced *with facts and figures* about the soundness of the venture, and it is well to remember that bank managers can be very tough when it comes to committing the funds of the bank to support the realization of your particular dream.

The simplest way of borrowing from a bank is by means of an overdraft which means your account can go into the red up to an agreed limit. This has the advantage that you are only paying interest on what you actually need at any particular time. However, the interest rate is not fixed and can vary with the bank base rate which can sometimes prove to be more expensive than anticipated. In addition, a bank can call in an overdraft at its discretion, although it rarely does so except in extreme circumstances. A bank providing an overdraft of such proportions will almost certainly expect the borrower to put in part of the necessary capital from personal resources. The bank will also expect some sort of security. If the business has considerable realizable assets of its own this may be sufficient, or the bank may require some independent guarantee.

Banks also provide both short- and medium-term loans, often tailored to the needs of the small business. The bank undertakes to lend a fixed sum to the borrower at a fixed rate of interest over the whole of the term and the borrower undertakes to pay the interest and repay the principal in set instalments over an agreed period. The disadvantage of this method is that it is less flexible than an overdraft but its advantage is a generally lower interest rate which will not vary throughout the period of the loan.

Capital can, of course, be raised privately if you can find an affluent relative or friend who is willing to come into partnership either as an active or a sleeping partner. However, as there can be many complications to a partnership it is essential when considering such a measure to seek professional advice and to ensure that every aspect of the matter is clearly understood and above all put down in writing.

There are schemes to help start up small businesses which have been initiated by the government and it may be beneficial to look into the possibility of financial aid offered by local and central government which include guaranteed overdrafts, subsidized rates and rents, and loans for the purchase of new equipment. The people who can point you in the right direction are your bank manager, the Manpower Services Commission, or an appropriate department of the local authority.

Buying an existing business

There are a number of advantages to buying a going concern provided it is sound in all important respects. The most obvious advantage is that it will have an established clientele which has been built up over a number of years. Thus revenue and hopefully adequate profits already exist. It is important to remember, however, that the existing custom was not built on your reputation and that it may well have been acquired as a direct result of a personality substantially different from your own and by applying methods which may not necessarily find favour in your eyes. Existing staff, which you may be wise to make every effort to retain, may not take kindly to a new boss or to changes which may be too many too soon. There is always the chance, of course, that they may breathe a sigh of relief to discover that you are perhaps a more efficient and more understanding employer than the last one.

Caveat emptor, or let the buyer beware, is an ancient rule which is well worth observing when considering any major purchase and most certainly when entering into the somewhat complicated process of buying a business.

Since it is not normally possible for the average individual to possess the specialized knowledge and experience necessary to assess the current value and future potential of such a business it is essential to proceed only with expert guidance. Of course you will know most things about your own particular field of activity in practical terms but this will be of little help in reading the signs which a solicitor or an accountant would instantly recognize as an indication that all may not be quite as it seems on the surface. Indeed the enthusiastic hairdresser or beauty therapist is most likely to see the matter mainly from the point of view of the practical and social skills of the trade whereas a solicitor will take a legal point of view and an accountant a financial point of view.

Existing staff and contracts of employment

It is as well to appreciate your position under employment law should you wish to dispense with the services of some of the existing staff. If a business is sold as a going concern it is reasonable to assume that contracts of employment in respect of existing staff may remain valid for the purposes of redundancy and that their service with the old employer may be added to that with the new employer to form one continuous period of employment. If the employer is a sole trader then any contract of employment is a personal one between that employer and the employee and would normally terminate should the business close down entirely or the employer dies, but if you buy the business as a going concern while that employer is still alive and you continue running it in the same place then it may be held that you have taken over the contracts of employment and the liabilities thereunder. If you intend to continue the employment then all is well but if you plan to make staff cuts it would be wise to ascertain at the outset your position with regard to periods of notice, fair dismissal, and redundancy payment liability.

Reasons for selling

It is important to know why the present owner is selling and that may mean finding the true reason which may be different from the one given.

The actual situation (site) of the business is important and it may quite simply be in the wrong place for the type of trade. This could mean the present level of trading is all or almost all it will ever achieve.

It can be argued that in these days of almost universal car ownership most clients can travel anywhere for a service they want. Unfortunately a car has to be left somewhere when it is not being driven – and being forced to park some distance away and walk to the salon could discourage many potential customers unless it happens to be a town-centre position where a hairdo or beauty treatment can be combined with some shopping or lunch. Remember that customers who may have found the situation inconvenient but continued their patronage out of a long-standing sense of loyalty could find a change of ownership affords an opportunity to make the break and go elsewhere. Change of ownership may, of course, provide an opportunity to break off the relationship for a variety of other reasons.

If existing staff are content to remain with the business and you are content to keep them, then provided any changes of policy are slowly and tactfully introduced there is no reason why most of the original custom should not remain also. Sometimes, however, a change of leadership can have an unsettling effect which results in a steady migration of staff.

Vetting the accounts

Because the sole trader is under no legal compulsion to keep accounts other than the minimum records necessary to satisfy the Inland Revenue it is possible that accounts which do exist may be of limited help in establishing the financial soundness of the business. A partnership is legally required to keep accounts but not required to have them audited. A limited company must not only keep full accounts but is also required to employ recognized auditors and have the accounts filed at Companies House where they are open to public inspection.

Properly kept accounts and records can tell much about the past and the present performance of the business but cannot foretell the future. For example, they will not necessarily reveal that the business may be at the peak of its potential for that particular catchment area or, on the other hand, that it has been under-exploited and the present volume of trading falls short of the possible maximum.

Ideally, accounts should be available to cover at least the last three financial years and the most important accounts to see are the:

* trading account;
* profit and loss account;
* balance sheet, together with a statement showing the sources and applications of funds.

It is important to be able to determine:

* costs of production against revenue from services/sales which gives the gross profit;
* overhead expenses against gross profit which gives the net profit;
* true value of fixed assets after depreciation;
* true value of stock, but beware redundant stock which became useless to the present owner and may prove to be equally useless to you should you buy it.

A good accountant will know exactly what to look for and you would be well advised to seek the services of such a person. Unless the accountant is thoroughly familiar with the valuation of a hairdressing or beauty therapy business he will probably want your opinion on the condition and usefulness of fittings, equipment and stock since you should be the best person to know about such things.

The assets

Both freehold and leasehold premises may be regarded as an asset of the business. A freehold is a more tangible asset but since it is unlikely that the average hairdresser or beauty therapist venturing into business for the first time would have sufficient capital available to purchase a freehold we will con-sider only leasehold premises.

The value of a lease as an asset will depend upon its terms and conditions and the length of its unexpired term. In all cases it is essential that the leasehold is transferable from the present tenant to you and from you to a future tenant should you wish to sell the business at a later date. It is also necessary to check rent review dates and date of renewal, together with tenant's specific liabilities. Your solicitor should automatically do all of this for you but it is as well to know what is necessary.

The main fixed assets will be furniture, fittings and equipment but it is unrealistic to evaluate these on the basis of their supposed market value. Resale values of used furniture, fittings and equipment can be low even when they are in good condition. Most of these items can only be valued in the light of their worth to the business as a going concern. Clearly anything which is likely to become worn out in the near future cannot be considered as a long-term asset.

Stock can be much more easily valued but once again account must be taken of its present and future worth to the services provided by the business. Deterioration through poor or over-long storage, or changes in popularity as a result of new fashion trends may already have rendered some of the stock useless or redundant.

Remember that the worth of a business is dependent upon its assets, for that is what you are buying. Of course there will also be certain liabilities which are part of the package deal, and nobody in their right mind would think of buying a liability, but provided they are not unreasonable they can be accepted as such. Assets can be divided into two categories:

1 *tangible assets* which include furniture, fittings and equipment, together with stock, all of which comprise the accoutrements and materials of the trade;
2 *intangible assets* which consist mainly of the existing custom and reputation of the business which together constitute the goodwill.

Goodwill

The goodwill of a business is the benefit which arises from its having been carried on for some time by a particular person and/or in particular premises. Goodwill is regarded as an intangible asset because the value consists merely in the probability that existing customers will continue to be customers regardless of a change of ownership. Goodwill represents the value of the attraction to customers or clients which the business name and reputation possesses. It represents an *anticipated value* over and above stock, equipment, fittings, furniture, lease or premises.

It is necessary to distinguish between *personal goodwill* which is attached to the present owner or proprietor of the business and often to some extent, as in the case of a hairdressing or beauty therapy business, to members of the operative staff, and *local goodwill* which is attached to familiar premises. In personal service businesses goodwill is much more likely to be closely associated with the relationships which exist between the people who actually carry out the services and the clients.

Protecting the goodwill. A person selling the goodwill along with the business undertakes with the purchaser, by implication, not to solicit clients existing prior to the sale. Thus the purchaser of the goodwill is given the opportunity to keep existing clients. Naturally if the new owner adopts policies which do not please those clients they may leave and the goodwill will thereby disappear through no fault on the part of the previous owner.

Clearly goodwill would be a worthless asset if it were not possible to protect it. In the absence of an express agreement the seller of the business goodwill is not prevented from setting up in competition elsewhere and may do everything that a stranger to the business sold would be in a position to do but must not take advantage of special knowledge of the old clientele to regain without consideration that which has been parted with for value. In other words the owner may not sell the custom and then steal away the customers. In law this matter can be extremely complex and it is always advisable when purchasing a business and goodwill to insist on a covenant whereby the previous owner either undertakes not to compete under a radius/time clause or at least undertakes not to take unreasonable steps to recover old custom.

Starting from scratch

Starting a new business is in many ways different from purchasing a going concern for nothing exists ready-made. Suitable premises must be found, planning permission considered and a lease negotiated. Next comes decor, fixtures, furniture, fittings, equipment, stock and not least advertising to tell people you are there and ready for business. Assuming you can raise the capital the amount needed may not be all that different to purchasing an existing business except in one essential respect and that is the need for *working capital*. A new business will have no ready-made revenue and even if you have some clients who will follow you into your new venture they are unlikely to be sufficient in number to meet all overhead expenses as well as costs of production. Therefore it is essential to have access to working capital sufficient to support the business and pay many of the bills during the early development period – which could mean several months at least before you break even or hopefully make a profit.

The main advantage of an entirely new business is that you will be able to build the business the way you want from the very start and create your own image from the outset. This does not mean you will necessarily be successful but if you are then you can truly say 'I did it my way'. The golden rule is not to be too positive in your attitudes but to be prepared to modify tactics particularly when there are clear signs that you have not yet got it quite right.

All business transactions involve at least an element of risk. A business can turn out to be less profitable than expected or even fail for reasons which could not have been foreseen no matter how thorough an investigation had been made.

A sensible and necessary precaution is to adopt a completely realistic attitude when proposing to take on a new commitment and to remember that things are rarely all that they may appear at first sight. It is all too easy to allow natural enthusiasm to override caution and common sense. It would, for example, be unwise to sign a lease or a binding agreement for a lease without a thorough personal inspection of the premises, or better still having a professional survey carried out; without looking at the surrounding area and the kinds of business already established; without considering ease of access to the premises and the availability of medium-stay parking for clients; without making formal enquiries at the local authority offices about any proposals that could directly or indirectly affect your business; without arranging for your solicitor to submit a local search and enquiry to the local authority and advise on the result; without arranging for your solicitor to submit enquiries before contract to the landlord's solicitor, or without ensuring that all necessary planning permissions, licences and consents from superior landlords or mortgagees have been obtained.

The lease

It is absolutely essential at the outset to settle the main terms of the tenancy. Remember there are more factors in a lease than the amount of rent to be paid. There are no standard terms for business premises and the landlord and tenant are entirely free to negotiate their own terms. No matter how keen you may be to start in business never accept a lease without having first properly understood all of its terms and conditions, preferably with the aid of professional advice. Remember that once the lease is signed the terms and conditions cannot normally be altered during the period for which it is intended to run no matter how inconvenient they may subsequently prove to be.

Today new business leases may be on a periodic basis running from year to year or even from month to month for a relatively short term of five or seven years. Any lease for more than five years is almost bound to contain provision for rent increases at given intervals. The tenant has a statutory right to apply for renewal of a lease but the right is subject to a number of exceptions under which the landlord could refuse to comply.

The main question is whether it is better to have a short-term or a long-term lease. The problem with a short-term lease is that it may not offer sufficient security. No one wants to spend five years building up a business and then be forced to move to other premises because the lease cannot be renewed. Some people are afraid of a long-term lease in case the business fails to prosper but that view hardly suggests confidence in the venture. Provided the terms and conditions of a long-term lease are on the whole favourable to the tenant it is better to work hard to make a success of the business on the basis of that security.

2 Capital

Every business needs capital. In the first instance, to finance its establishment and subsequently to support future development. Capital is generally defined under three headings:

* *capital owned*, which is the credit balance of the capital account, the financial holding or equity in the case of the sole trader;
* *capital employed*, which is the total amount of fixed and current assets at the disposal of and for the full use and benefit of the business;
* *working capital*, which is simply cash directly or indirectly available to meet the costs and expenses of day-to-day trading activities.

The accountant's view of capital

Most people think of capital as something a business or company has got – something it *owns*. Why then does it appear on the liability side of the balance sheet, together with a bank loan and any other source of finance which is owed? This is because accountants think of capital in a negative way as something the business or company *owes*.

A moment's thought will show that a sole trader business owes private capital to the owner and a company owes share capital to the shareholders, just as a loan is owed to the bank and trade debts to trade creditors.

Sources of capital

There are three main ways in which capital is acquired:

* private finance, which is provided by the owner at the outset and sometimes simply referred to as capital but is more correctly *owner's capital*,

* finance derived from the issue of shares in a company, which is known as *share capital*,
* finance obtained by borrowing by one means or another, which is known as *loan or debt capital*.

Gearing

A sole trader business has two fundamentally different sources of capital, namely:

* owner's capital which includes net profit as retained earnings;
* loan or debt capital, which is money borrowed by the business from outside sources.

When a business has a high proportion of outside money to inside money this is referred to as *high gearing*. It is desirable that the ratio of gearing should never be more than 1:1, that is 50 per cent owner's capital to 50 per cent debt capital. High gearing increases the cost and the risk to the business while low gearing decreases the cost and the risk.

Capital and revenue

At this point it will be useful to distinguish between capital and revenue.

Revenue is derived from trading activities and is used mainly to finance those activities by paying current costs and expenses. If revenue consistently fails to do this the business cannot be said to be paying its way.

Revenue provides the greater part of working capital but there are occasions when additional finance is required on an essentially temporary basis, for example:

* a new business which is not yet generating sufficient revenue to meet all of its trading liabilities;
* a business where a period of time may elapse between carrying out the work and receipt of cash in final settlement of the account.

The latter example applies particularly to manufacturing and some service industries where it is necessary to cover the cost of work in progress, but should not normally concern a hairdressing or beauty therapy business provided extensive credit is not given.

Credit control

A business which supplies goods and/or services on credit must exercise credit control to ensure that current cash revenue is sufficient to meet current costs and expenses, otherwise it may be necessary to lean heavily on additional working capital for support.

Raising loan or debt capital

Whether you are considering entering the business world for the first time by opening an entirely new business or purchasing an existing one, or developing some aspect of a business you already own, the greatest limiting factor is likely to be a shortage of money.

Clearly in the case of an entirely new venture, or buying a going concern you must already have some cash or convertible assets to put up a reasonable proportion of the finance required.

If you own an established and already successful business it should have been possible with careful planning and foresight to have built up capital reserves over the intervening years by the investment of surplus profits, but even this may prove to be insufficient to fund a proposed expansion or new development entirely on its own.

It is patently obvious that it will be much more expensive to borrow money than to use your own and it is essential to be sure that there is in fact no spare cash or convertible asset available in your business or in your private means.

When considering borrowing additional money, probably the first thought that comes to mind is a bank. Banks are probably better placed than most institutions to understand the needs and problems of the small business for indeed many thousands of small businesses are numbered among their customers. Bank managers are however both experienced and realistic when it comes to lending money and will need to be convinced of the soundness of your proposition and your ability to meet the commitments involved. If you already have a well-managed account this will help a great deal. It need not be a large account simply bulging with money for if that were the case you probably would not need to borrow money. The important thing is to have built up a record of good financial management. If your account has tended to move from overdrawn to affluence and back to overdrawn with monotonous frequency then it would be reasonable to suppose you do not manage your financial affairs very well. The bank manager will not be impressed by great inspirational ideas but will want to see well prepared facts and figures which show that you have considered every foreseeable factor. Remember that you are asking the bank to take risks with money which indirectly represents deposits belonging to other customers. If your venture fails and you have insufficient assets to clear the debt the bank may have to write it off as a loss and the manager's superiors will want to know why he agreed to lend the money in the first instance.

Do not overlook the fact that during the term of the loan you will not only be expected to regularly pay back a proportion of the principal but also quite a substantial sum in the form of interest. In addition you may be expected to match the bank's loan by putting in at least some cash of your own. A bank is much more likely to be prepared to meet a shortfall than to put up all of the money needed.

While a bank may be prepared to agree to a short-term loan of a modest sum without security in the case of an established and responsible customer, all larger medium-term loans will certainly require some kind of collateral.

Perhaps the most common source of modest short-term finance for use in business is the overdraft and this is generally the least expensive way of obtaining money from an outside source mainly because interest is charged only on the out-standing debit balance of your account. Even so there is some-thing slightly demoralizing about a bank account which seems to be permanently in the red. In addition this is not a fixed-term loan and this means that it lies within the discretion of the bank manager to call in the whole of the outstanding amount at any time should he consider it advisable. The manager will also want to know for what purpose the money is required before he agrees to provide the overdraft facility.

A relative or friend might be prepared to help solve your financial problem but it is only fair to say you should never borrow money from either of them unless they actually do not need it and could perhaps wait quite a long time for repayment or even afford to lose it should you fail.

Finally, *never borrow from a money lender* whose primary aim in life is to ensure that you take the longest possible time to pay off the principal and so add more and more to his already considerable wealth by continuing to pay the very high interest charged.

Within the limited compass of this book it has been possible only to touch upon the simplest basis of borrowing. Initially the best course is to consult your bank manager who will certainly give you good advice and if you are sufficiently convincing perhaps the money as well.

3
The salon

It is not usual for business premises designated as shops to be constructed with a particular trade in mind. Therefore, at the outset shop premises generally consist of so many square feet of floor space with the usual offices attached. This space may be oblong, square or irregular and how this is utilized will depend largely upon the tenant and the shopfitter. Anything involving structural alterations to the premises will generally require a landlord's consent and perhaps planning permission also.

Clearly the nature of the business will have considerable influence on what is required. A hairdressing salon will probably concentrate on as much open space as possible whereas a beauty therapy salon will need some areas of partial privacy for some of its services and complete privacy for others.

Whereas in the old days all hairdressing salons were constructed on a private cubicle system, which had the disadvantage of restricting the number of clients which could be taken at any one time the modern salon favours the open system which makes the maximum use of available space and allows a greater volume of custom to pass through.

The internal layout of a salon should be planned to provide a balance between appearance, comfort, efficiency and maximum productivity. The layout must take into account the needs of the staff, the comfort, well-being and satisfaction of the clients, and lastly the financial prosperity of the business.

In both hairdressing and beauty therapy salons the clients will spend quite some time passively submitting to the various processes. In these circumstances it is essential that they should be comfortable and equally important that they should not become bored. The siting of equipment where waiting is necessary should aim at providing an attractive and/or interesting outlook for those who have to do the waiting and that does not mean looking at a blank wall a few paces away. A display of attractive pictures and/or amusing cartoons would make an acceptable alternative to staring at a plain white surface –

and these could be changed from time to time to maintain interest.

Productive and non-productive areas

Productive areas directly earn money while non-productive areas do not, and although some non-productive areas are unavoidable they should not be allowed to take up more space than absolutely necessary for the needs and comfort of those who use them. A spacious reception area can provide an attractive first impression for new clients but it may be an uneconomic luxury if it is achieved at the expense of much-needed working positions in the salon itself. A smaller reception area can also be attractive and comfortable provided it is not allowed to become overcrowded with waiting clients.

It is all a matter of proportion, of striking a realistic balance between the amount of space needed to accommodate waiting clients and that required for carrying out the actual services which produce the salon revenue. It is essential that careful consideration should be given to the possible consequences of overcrowding. This must be avoided at all costs for the sake of client and staff comfort, working efficiency and not least in the interests of health and safety. There are certain statutory requirements regarding working space. In addition, over-crowding is not only likely to increase health hazards and fire evacuation difficulties but may also cause mental as well as physical discomfort for claustrophobic clients. There will be some who will not mind a little togetherness but others may be completely put off by such conditions.

Salon layout and fire risk

It is essential that all premises should comply with fire regulations even when exempt from the necessity to obtain a fire certificate. It is an obvious duty of management to ensure that clients and staff can be evacuated from the premises in the shortest possible time in the event of fire or in any other dangerous situation. It should be borne in mind that while there is a common tendency to think of fire risk in terms of the people employed, that risk obviously extends to all persons who may be on the premises. Therefore, such precautions as are necessary and the process of evacuation should take into account the maximum number of persons who may be on the premises at any one time. Your local fire department will readily advise you with regard to your own particular salon.

Avoiding bottlenecks

It is important that consideration should be given to the layout of salon equipment so as not to unnecessarily delay evacuation. Fittings and equipment should be sited so as to allow free passage and doorways should allow easy exit. A trial evacuation or two will quickly show where problems might occur.

Utilization of space for maximum productivity

It will make a useful exercise for owners/managers of existing salons to study the extent to which effective use is being made of the available space, that is, reception, the operative salon itself, dispensary, laundry, stockroom, staffroom and so on. Measure the floor area of each of these and bearing in mind that only the actual operative salon is directly productive, compare the operative salon floor space figure with the combined figures for the remainder and you may be surprised to find that little more than, or even less than, one-half of the total floor space is directly productive. Now divide your total overheads by the number of square feet of operative salon floor space only and you will see how much it is costing per square foot of directly productive floor space to provide the revenue just to run your business.

It may not be possible to do much to gain extra productive floor space without making structural alterations but it may be worthwhile to look into the matter with a view to some less drastic changes.

One thing that can often be done with little extra expense is to look carefully at the layout of equipment and the passage of clients from one stage to another. Any client who is waiting for a process to develop while occupying a position which may be required by another client can cause delay. An obvious example would be a client remaining seated at a shampoo position during the neutralizing of a permanent wave while another client waits to be shampooed. A simple solution to such a problem is to provide standby positions not involving

An impressive and spacious salon allowing considerable freedom of movement.

needed equipment. Naturally one would assume that the original equipping of the salon took into account foreseeable
needs but as in the case of our roads and motorways demand
can increase so rapidly as to outstrip the anticipations of those
who plan and prove quite inadequate in the long term.

The salon environment

Almost everyone will have their own ideas with regard to the
ideal social, domestic or business environment. Some people
like a quiet, calm atmosphere with a sense of order while
others crave movement and even noise. Some appreciate living
in a rural area whereas others would not live anywhere but in a
town. We take pleasure according to our individual tastes and
what is a joy to one could be a bore to another; what is exciting
to you could be stressful to someone else. The point is that no
one is necessarily wrong and in our private and personal lives
at least we are entitled to do our own thing provided, of
course, that exercise of individual freedom to please ourselves
does not deny an equal degree of freedom to others who may
think differently. When it comes to a business environment,
however, a particular problem arises. Here it is not simply a
question of establishing an environment to please ourselves
but to try to please the many and often very varied clients who
may frequent the salon. Therefore because it is scarcely possible to please everyone it is necessary to consider very carefully:

* What is likely to please, *or more importantly not to offend*,
  the potential clients available to you?
* What kind of custom do you wish to attract?

Here the expression 'salon environment' is used in a broad
sense and can comprise many factors. The total salon environment will include within the layout of the premises and management of the business:

fixtures, fittings, furnishings, equipment, decor, lighting, heating, ventilation, noise level, personal facilities for the clients,
working practices, staff facilities, staff appearances and social
attitudes.

Some clients will adapt to a situation and accept the status quo
and will not be over-sensitive to other factors provided the end
result of the service meets with their approval but others will
have quite definite expectations with regard to the environment in which the services are carried out.

In present-day marketing, packaging is of considerable importance and many manufacturers spend a great deal of money in order to ensure that their products are presented in the most effective way. Clearly many people are at least initially encouraged to purchase a particular product by its attractive packaging.

How well do you package your product? Whether it is a hairdressing service or a beauty therapy service – your salon and its environment represent the packaging or presentation of the services you offer.

The salon decor

The visual aspect of a salon which is likely to make the most immediate impact on the public is the decor and it is in this respect that tastes will almost certainly differ widely. Therefore, it is a great mistake to ignore this fact by imposing your personal preference upon them. In general the answer is to go in for a colour scheme which is attractive but not intrusive. Not everyone will appreciate strong bold colours or bizarre designs even if they are fashionable and so it is not so much a question of what will please but rather *what will not offend*. A relatively subdued scheme providing an effective background to some brighter features such as curtain fabrics or furniture covers, pictures and flowers is likely to be generally acceptable. A background should never dominate otherwise it ceases to perform the function of a background.

Furniture

Furniture essentially needs to be functional and at the same time comfortable. Also in the interests of economy it must be strong and long-lasting. Bear in mind that clients come in all shapes and sizes and that the same items of furniture must accommodate all of them without discomfort. Working items of furniture such as shampoo chairs and dressing chairs must be totally adjustable to meet the needs and comfort of the operatives. Both hairdressers and beauty therapists can suffer from back problems and poorly designed salon furniture and equipment can be a contributory cause.

Equipment

The primary requirement for equipment is that it should be functional, efficient and reliable in the long term. If equipment

A useful stand-by group of dryers in a convenient position.

can at the same time present an attractive and/or interesting appearance that is an added advantage.

Because of the wide range of furniture and equipment now available it is not possible to even attempt to make recommendations in these pages except to say that it always pays to consult specialist manufacturers and/or suppliers who will be only too pleased to give you the benefit of their experience.

Lighting and heating

Adequate lighting in the salon is of greatest importance and the colour character of the light is equally significant. It is not too difficult to appreciate that the effect of a white surface under an orange or a red light will appear warmer and under a blue or violet light will appear cooler. Equally the effect of a coloured surface will often be modified by the type of light falling upon it. Different types of lighting often exhibit different colour characteristics and it is important to determine beforehand what effect any proposed lighting will have on the general decor of the salon and even more importantly what effect it will have on the skin and/or hair of the clients. It is also important to recognize that local colour schemes such as the colour of the walls and other surfaces as well as the colour of fabrics will contribute to the general lighting effect by absorbing and/or reflecting colour components of light.

Light is vital to the visual process and particularly to colour vision. It is difficult to see effectively in low light conditions and virtually impossible to do so in complete darkness. The intensity as well as the colour quality of light is essential to the perception of subtle colour differences because whereas black and white is relatively easily identifiable in low light conditions it is extremely difficult if not impossible to determine subtle colour differences in the same circumstances. In recent years it has become fashionable to use spotlights for both business and domestic lighting. While the use of such devices can increase light intensity in a given area there can be two distinct disadvantages for the hairdresser or beauty therapist, which are:

* if the light source has an unsuitable colour character it can have considerable effect on the perceived colour of hair and/or skin;
* if a high wattage light source is used the beam can transmit heat which can affect the development of a process and/or cause a degree of discomfort for operative and/or client.

Space heating. Space heating in the salon must be efficient, adequate under extreme conditions and at the same time totally controllable in order to avoid an overheated atmosphere.

It is essential to maintain an optimum comfortable temperature bearing in mind that what may be comfortable for busy members of staff may be quite cool to the static client, particularly when her hair is wet. Room thermostats placed at strategic points are an absolute necessity and care should be taken to maintain an evenly balanced temperature throughout the salon. Normal central heating, or electric storage heaters, are suitable but any system using open flame gas heaters directly in the salon whether to provide space heating or hot water can have the disadvantage of producing excess water vapour with resulting condensation.

Humidity. Hairdressing salons in particular are prone to high levels of humidity due to the nature of some of the processes and the often large number of people present in the relatively small space of the operative salon. Relative humidity in a salon which is too high is a clear indication of inadequate ventilation and can result in a tendency to tiredness, irritability, even headache and dizziness, in addition to increasing the possibility of the transmission of air-borne infections. For optimum comfort the relative humidity should not rise above 50 per cent and it is worthwhile to instal a hygrometer to keep a check on this.

Ventilation. Ventilation and space heating really need to be considered together. Too little ventilation can result in overheating and too much can waste money by reducing the effectiveness of the heating system. In order to ensure a healthy atmosphere and optimum comfort it is necessary to maintain a balance between the two. Clients and staff will affect the composition of the air in the salon by reducing oxygen and increasing carbon dioxide, water vapour and bacterial content. Under normal circumstances this should not cause too many problems provided the atmosphere is prevented from becoming static by a ventilation system capable of completely changing the air over a reasonable period of time.

Too rapid movement of air should be avoided because this can cause draughts. Warm air escaping through a ventilator will cause cool air to be drawn in through any available inlet, generally at a lower level such as the space beneath a door. Floor draughts are the most commonly forgotten possibility. Warm air rises to escape at the highest point and cooler air

A more traditional double-sided dressing unit without accompanying wall-mounted dryers.

enters at the lowest point causing a cold floor. Avoid cold floors in your salon by providing good insulating covering.

Natural ventilation. The old-fashioned sash window opened at the bottom to let cooler air in and at the top to allow warmer air to escape, thus assisting the behaviour of convection currents which contribute to changing the air in a room. Since that time various other ventilation devices have been produced which make for more or less efficient and controllable natural ventilation. The key to natural ventilation is the provision of an inlet as well as an outlet. Opening the top ventilator in your kitchen while cooking will not be truly effective unless there is also a suitable inlet on the other side of the room (preferably low down) to allow replacement air to create the necessary movement. In the salon it is not generally sufficient to rely upon natural ventilation and the adequate movement of air will require some assistance.

Artificially assisted ventilation. The simplest form of assisted ventilation consists of suitable extractor fans situated in windows or in external walls. Today many people use such a device in their homes but it should be borne in mind that to be really effective it is necessary to provide a suitably placed inlet. In the salon it is important to have inlets positioned at points farthest from the extractor fans to allow a current of air to flow through. Fans can also be used at the inlets to draw in fresh air and so provide a combination of assisted inlets and outlets to allow greater control of air movement throughout the salon. The ultimate luxury is, of course, an air-conditioning installation which can filter and clean the air, adjust its humidity and either cool or warm the air before re-entry, but that would be something the majority of salons could not afford.

Once again the best course is to consult the specialists in the field who will have the technology and the instrumentation to carry out tests and advise on the most appropriate type of installation.

Laundry and salon cleaning

Laundering facilities are a necessity and can best be provided by the installation of a suitable washing machine and tumble-dryer, preferably in a separate room because a washing machine can be noisy and a tumble-dryer not only noisy but prone to heat the air around it.

A busy salon can get through a considerable number of

towels during the course of a single day and, of course, gowns need to be washed regularly.

Some salons use junior staff to do this work but where the demand is considerable this is not fair on the juniors who are supposed to be learning their trade and indeed this may not be strictly within the implied terms of their contract.

The most efficient and desirable way of dealing with laundering needs is to employ a non-hairdressing member of staff who could be engaged even on a part-time basis to combine this duty with general cleaning duties in the salon. Cleaning must be carried out on a regular basis and while junior staff could reasonably be expected to help out by maintaining general tidiness they should not be asked to do any of the main cleaning. Where laundry and cleaning are casually done by whoever happens to be free this can lead to temporary neglect of these very necessary chores during times when all of the hairdressing staff are needed to give service to the clients. Some operative staff may be willing to assist in an emergency but apart from any other reason it would not be cost-effective to use them to carry out this relatively unskilled work on a regular basis.

Stockroom and dispensary

Larger salons carrying a considerable volume of stock will benefit from a stockroom where these items can be kept secure and transferred in controllable quantities to a dispensing area. A small salon with limited space available may have to be content with a large cupboard which can be similarly safe-guarded and again stock transferred to a separate dispensing area. In either case the dispensing area should be equipped with sink and drainer together with waste bins, storage shelves and dispensing equipment.

A suggested method of stock control will be found in Chapter 13 under Stock records and Dispensary.

Refreshments for clients

Any manager already providing or contemplating providing food and/or drink for consumption by clients in the salon should bear in mind that this service will be subject to Food Hygiene regulations enforced by the local authority through their Environmental Health Department. A simple cup of coffee or tea and a biscuit should not present too many problems in this respect provided an adequate standard of hygiene is maintained. The use of an approved drinks dispensing machine will

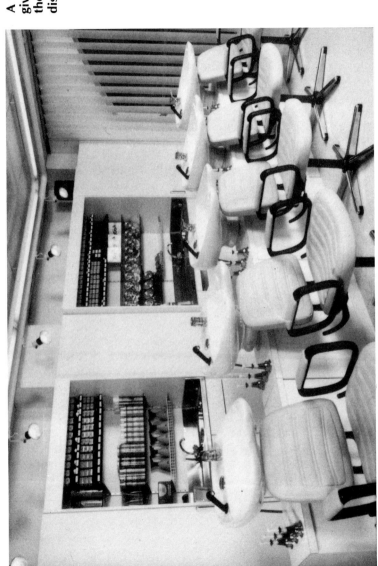

A free-standing basin run giving staff easy access to the well-equipped dispensing area.

meet the requirements because the cups or beakers are clean and new to begin with and disposable when they have been used. On no account should they be reused. This method suffers from the disadvantage that it is not a particularly attractive way of presenting the beverage and is not always of the most palatable quality. Since, however, most people are now apparently accustomed to this departure from gracious living it should prove to be reasonably acceptable. To provide anything more sophisticated will inevitably take up staff time, require suitable crockery, an appropriate system of cleansing and adequate equipment for the preparation of the drinks.

Toilet facilities for clients

Adequate toilet facilities should be provided for use by clients and it is essential that they should be scrupulously clean and hygienic. A toilet tissue dispenser and a spare roll of tissue is obviously necessary but a toilet brush should also be provided to encourage cleanliness. Decor should be attractive and there should be both adequate ventilation and a means of counteracting offensive odours. A hand basin with a soap dispenser and disposable hand towels is also a necessity. A suitable waste bin with disposable plastic liner should be provided. Unless it is absolutely unavoidable it is not a good thing at any time to allow staff and clients to share the same toilet facilities.

Staff facilities

Ideally staff facilities should comprise a rest room with the means to prepare light refreshments, a changing room or rooms with personal lockers and separate toilet or toilets. Toilets should be no less well equipped than those provided for clients.

Salon maintenance

This is not just a matter of maintaining working equipment but caring for everything which contributes to a high standard of service. Apart from the economic advantage of keeping fixtures, fittings, furniture and equipment in good order, proper maintenance also makes an essential contribution to the health and safety of clients and staff. There are many circumstances in which failure to take immediate action to make good a fault could lead to an accident and a possible subsequent claim for damages on the grounds of negligence.

The most obvious example concerns the regular inspection and checking of all electrical points and equipment to ensure they are safe to use. Another instance could be failure to make good damaged floor covering which could result in a client sustaining injury through falling, and yet one more example could be failure to replace immediately a failed light on a staircase with similar results. Bear in mind that while there may be adequate insurance to cover such an event and even though negligence may not necessarily be proven there is still the matter of adverse publicity which could affect public confidence.

Maintenance also applies to the visual appearance of the salon and the comfort of the clientele. Decor which is obviously marked and/or fading, upholstery and fabrics fraying at the edges, floor covering which is past its best, equipment which is falling apart, together with towels and gowns in obvious need of replacement will make it clear that maintenance is not a high priority. Some people may hardly notice such things but there will always be those who do and they are the ones who will probably take their custom elsewhere and worse still talk about it.

Cleanliness is of paramount importance, together with the maintenance of a high standard of hygiene. Constant vigilance is essential because people are not always aware of their own unhygienic practices. For example, if a canteen instals steam equipment for the sterilization of cups – a good idea in principle – the whole object can be defeated by allowing staff to transfer cleansed cups from their sterilizing trays by placing fingers inside them.

In a hairdressing salon the cleanliness of shampoo basins is of great importance and it is not just a matter of keeping a clean surface. Traps and waste pipes should be kept clear, free-flowing and regularly disinfected. Traps are fitted to maintain a water seal which will prevent airborne bacteria and unpleasant odours from returning from the drains and they should be kept clear of hair and other debris. The worst enemy of the waste water system in a hairdressing salon is a combination of loose hair and natural grease forming a plug which will slow down and even stop altogether the flow of water. In most cases regular clearing with a caustic preparation (sodium hydroxide) is necessary.

The disposal of an ever-increasing volume of waste material poses a growing problem in the modern world and constantly threatens the natural environment. The primary waste material in hairdressing is cut hair and while this is not exactly an environmental risk it can constitute a health and safety hazard if left carelessly lying around. Tiny particles of hair can float around in air currents and be unknowingly breathed in. It is now suspected that in the days when barbers carried out hundreds of finely graduated haircuts (short-back-and-sides) the minute bits of hair which flew off were partly breathed in and may have been a contributory cause of respiratory problems later in life. Again, even the smallest amount of hair left lying on the floor could cause a client or a member of staff to slip and fall. Hair, loose particles of skin and general dust can lie on work surfaces and to this mixture on the floor can be added material brought in on the shoes of the clients. Clearly, strict cleanliness is essential and the avoidance of cleaning methods which could lift this noxious brew into the atmosphere.

Efficient laundering of all towels, gowns and other non-disposable items is absolutely essential, together with the hygienic collection and storage of used items prior to laundering. Disposable materials are of great value where close contact with the skin of the client is concerned and it should be remembered that the operative word is *disposable*, which means you do not leave them lying around but dispose of them right away. One objection to people who use tissues instead of a handkerchief is their tendency to discard them almost anywhere without realizing, or perhaps not caring about, the health risk they may pose to other people.

Reception

The reception area of a hotel, a hairdressing salon, a beauty therapy salon, a suite of offices, even a hospital can be regarded as the first personal point of contact with the organization. One dictionary definition of reception is 'the receiving or welcoming of persons as visitors formally or ceremoniously'. In the context of business, however, reception needs to be rather more than merely being nice to clients, answering enquiries or booking appointments. Ideally, reception regulates and controls access to the next stage in a procedure. The hairdressing or beauty therapy operative will carry out the practical work but the service begins and ends in reception.

The personality of the receptionist is of paramount importance and knowledge, understanding and efficiency equally so. First-class receptionists are relatively rare and, generally, worth their weight in gold. As with many other occupations it is

A modern reception area with elegant simplicity in design.

doubtful if all of the skills of a good receptionist can actually be learned. There are some intangible qualities which cannot be easily defined and for this and other reasons cannot actually be taught. The practicalities of reception could be carried out by most people but the finer points are elusive and therefore reception is not really a job for any member of staff who happens to be free at the time. In many salons a full-time receptionist is not an economic possibility and so of necessity it has to be done by junior staff or shared between fully qualified members of staff. Using fully qualified members of staff for work which is not directly productive can be uneconomic and junior members do not generally know enough about the services to carry out some reception functions efficiently.

Ideally, the post of receptionist should be a full-time appointment and the person concerned should preferably have at least an adequate basic knowledge of all of the services provided. However, the right personality is the foremost requirement and intensive training could be provided to familiarize that person with the nature of the processes and their implications as a service to the public. Since reception involves management of people, social skills and some management skills are also necessary. To be truly effective the receptionist, like a good private secretary, must have an adequate general understanding of the day-to-day running of the business. It is a curious fact that whereas many salons recognize the importance of on-going training for their operative staff very few appear to be aware that this is also a need in terms of reception. We are all aware of the poor service we sometimes receive at the hands of shop assistants who clearly have never had any effective sort of training in how to maintain good relationships with the general public. We have also experienced the very different atmosphere in an establishment where the management values good service and a good public image and make every effort to ensure that staff are carefully selected and properly trained to preserve that image.

While reception is important in even the smallest salon it can be crucial in the larger establishment which has many members of staff and offers a wide range of services. Reception should be regarded as part of management and where it is well done the receptionist deserves proper recognition.

Not everyone is a suitable candidate for the post of receptionist and indeed many who may make good operative hairdressers or beauty therapists may not possess the most suitable personality or have the inclination for this kind of work. Reception is just not for everyone and at its best only for a few.

Practical skills of reception

Almost anyone could be trained to meet the practical requirements of reception. The two most obvious points which come to mind are the need to be able to book appointments correctly and to be able to receive and record payments made by clients with similar accuracy. Although you may instal a first-class system, in actual practice it will only be as good as the person who operates it. In short, it may be fool proof but is it damn fool proof? Never put an inexperienced person on reception and just leave them to get on with it. It is clearly the responsibility of management to ensure that nothing is left to chance. Proper initial training and a subsequent period of supervision is essential.

It is important to operate a reasonably safe and efficient system for storage and retrieval of clients' outdoor clothing and possibly any personal belongings that would be inconvenient to carry with them throughout the salon processes.

There should be a method of identification such as numbered hangers for items of clothing where the number is entered against the appointment in the book on arrival and the garment(s) easily retrieved on departure. The worst kind of thing that can happen, and it is not uncommon, is for the receptionist to ask the client 'which coat is yours madam'. Even such a simple system as numbered hangers requires a disciplined approach on the part of receptionist to ensure that hangers are returned to their correct number sequence and the entry in the book is cancelled at the same time.

Reception should never be left unattended and only the receptionist on duty should have access to clients' property left in her charge. It is advisable, of course, to display a notice warning that all such items are left there at the owner's own risk.

Reception should have an air of alertness with instant attention for the clients on entry and yet should be calm and controlled. Remember that reception is more than the place where existing clients enter and depart, it is also the place of information for potential clients. If that information is not given accurately and presented in the right manner a new client could be lost.

Last but not least everything must be clean and tidy at all times. If a client has to wait there is no reason why she should not do so in a pleasant environment. Do not forget that the waiting client will have time to absorb the atmosphere, observe what goes on and if she has to wait long may become more critical of what she sees and hears.

Social skills of reception

The majority of those who enter reception will be quite ordinary people who respond favourably to courteous treatment. They will have different personalities and often different expectations with regard to the manner in which they would like to be treated. There is, however, one thing for certain that the more assertive will expect as of right and the others will gratefully appreciate and that is *prompt and interested attention from the receptionist*. Not a bored and laconic approach; not an irritable 'I can only attend to one person at a time' approach; not an over-effusive approach which is clearly not sincere but, in a word, a *professional* approach.

Almost everyone likes to feel at least just a little bit important and even strangers do not like to feel they are strangers. It is important to try to remember clients, even those who perhaps have only been once before and it is equally important to treat totally new clients with similar friendly courtesy. Remember that the aim is to build a mutually rewarding relationship with the clients and that it all begins with reception.

Once an enquiry has been satisfactorily answered and the appointment booked it is not a difficult matter to close the conversation with, for example, 'Thank you Mrs Brown, we look forward to seeing you at 10 o'clock on the 16th of October'. Mrs Brown will, of course, have been given an appointment card but this remark confirms the time and date in her mind and the *look forward to seeing you* leaves her with pleasant anticipation of the service to come.

When a client with an appointment has been verified in the book and the nature of the service confirmed it is the responsibility of the receptionist to ensure her comfort and well-being until she is transferred to the salon. The client should be gently assisted with the removal of outdoor clothing and perhaps gowned as necessary in readiness for treatment. Because a gown is not always an attractive garment some salons prefer not to apply gowns at this stage but to do so away from reception, especially if it is exposed to public view through the shop window. While this fine point would mean little to some people it could be important to others who are particularly sensitive about appearances.

Training for reception duties

Training in the practical skills of reception is a relatively clear-cut matter. In this instance we are not concerned with the personality of the receptionist but with the ability to learn and carry out predetermined procedures. Obviously it will be necessary to be able to deal effectively with telephone calls and make correct bookings by this means.

A good telephone manner is important and the receptionist should be able to speak clearly and concisely in a warm and pleasant voice. It is all too easy to be misunderstood and make mistakes over the telephone and to avoid this the receptionist needs an alert mind and an ability to concentrate on the matter in hand. Face to face contact in the reception area is easier and less prone to error because in this instance we can have total communication whereas over the telephone there is only the voice and that can be altered by the technology of the system. Some people unconsciously adopt a telephone manner which can be quite different to their normal approach. Therefore it is useful and sometimes quite revealing to listen attentively to the receptionist using the telephone in reception and then later call the salon number from an outside telephone and carry on a short conversation with the receptionist. There is no need to be secretive about it but reveal who you are if your voice has not in fact already been recognized and ask a few questions about this and that just to see how the response comes across. Incidentally, if the receptionist does immediately recognize your voice that is a good point in her favour because it shows she is alert and has a good aural memory.

No matter how apparently efficient the chosen system of booking may be in theory, in practice it will only be as good as the person who operates it. Beware the receptionist who ignores what may appear to her to be unnecessary work even though it is laid down in the procedure. This is most likely to happen during very busy times and could lead to unforeseen difficulties later on. It is, for example, essential that all appointments should be confirmed in writing on an appropriate appointment card. Such confirmation should include the nature of the service booked together with the day, date and time of the appointment. If the appointment is booked over the telephone the receptionist should repeat this information clearly and tactfully suggest that the caller should write it down.

Some salons make a practice of writing appointments in the book in pencil to allow for alterations and cancellations or for other reasons. This is unwise and could lead to mistakes through accidental rubbing out. It is much safer to write all appointments in ink and make corrections by applying self-adhesive stickers of the type that can be gently peeled off to reveal the writing underneath.

The chosen system for dealing with clients' outdoor clothing and with service gowns must be clearly understood and operated consistently. A careless or lazy receptionist could, for example, render a numbering system ineffective simply by failing to return hangers in their correct numerical order or failing to record the number against the appropriate entry in the appointment book.

It is obvious that the efficient handling of money is required and that honesty is essential. Accurate recording of all financial transactions is necessary and a system which is almost impossible to falsify will discourage any tendency to be light-fingered.

Dealing with the social skills of reception is not quite so simple a matter. This is not specifically training so much as a process of adapting an already suitable personality to the needs of the business with perhaps the correction of minor faults here or there. In short, building on qualities which are already present. Some are naturally good at showing care and understanding when dealing with people. Provided this attitude is sincere and consistent it would be unwise and indeed undesirable to tamper with it too much otherwise the result could appear artificial and contrived. Observe the receptionist in action and note how effectively these personal social skills, which may be innate and/or as a result of home and family influence, are applied to various clients, and most importantly how the clients react. Clearly if the clients are obviously happy you should be content on the whole to leave well alone. All that then remains is to ensure equal skill in the practical aspects of reception and the keeping of accurate records.

It is possible to encourage courteous and considerate attitudes in those who are apparently not naturally so endowed and sometimes development is so satisfactory as to suggest that the warmth of the true personality has been previously suppressed by other people and events. We are all subject to influences and pressures exerted by others and we are all to some extent at the mercy of our environment at any one time. Given care, time and a willingness to take a calculated risk you could eventually find that you have at least one employee who started doubtfully but ultimately became a valuable member of staff.

The communication link

The receptionist performs an essential function as the first communication link with the clients and should also provide an efficient communication link between clients in reception and operative staff in the salon. It is important that operative staff should have confidence in the ability of the receptionist and equally important that the receptionist recognizes the special knowledge and skills of the operative staff and can be relied upon to consult them when necessary. A receptionist is hardly likely to be popular with members of operative staff who have to cope with a badly organized working day as a direct result of incompetence in booking appointments.

Where operatives' commission is concerned it is important that the volume of work should be fairly allocated. Returning clients will generally go to their usual operative (personal clientele) but new clients who express no particular preference must be shared equally. There is also the question of personal optimum speed of working which can vary from one operative to another. Just one extra appointment squeezed in may cause great difficulty for one operative wheras another may handle it without too much trouble. Over the course of time the receptionist should be able to gain an intimate knowledge of the strengths and weaknesses of individual operatives which should make it possible to tactfully guide the flow of appointments in the interests of maximum productivity with minimum stress. Clearly this implies close cooperation between receptionist and operatives and a mutual trust and confidence which enables them to work as a team in the best interests of the business and all who are employed therein. It is again worth considering whether this happy state might be more readily achieved by replacing individual commission with a percentage profit-sharing scheme which offered overall productivity benefits to everyone concerned.

4 The role of the manager

It would be unreasonable to assume that every individual is capable of adapting to any situation. No two people are exactly alike and as personalities differ so also do aptitudes. For this reason alone there will inevitably be some things we can do well and some we cannot no matter how hard we may try. The individual hairdresser or beauty therapist may be happy following the practical aspects of their craft and yet find the rather different skills and responsibilities of management uninteresting and even stressful.

A large commercial enterprise would have access to legal advisers, accountants, market researchers, production managers, personnel managers and many others with specialist knowledge and experience. For the small business, especially in the beginning, it is much more likely to be a do-it-yourself affair. Unfortunately the skilled and successful operative with an ambition to go into business may later discover little liking or aptitude for the routine chores of management.

At least in the beginning the working proprietor will need, may even wish, to devote most or all of the time during open hours to giving personal practical service to the clientele. In such a case the paper work will almost certainly have to be dealt with after normal hours. Inevitably, as the business grows and staff increases the pressure to make a choice between the demands of management and working on the public will grow also. Eventually the answer will have to be one of delegation. But what and how much to delegate? This immediately raises a second question – what would be the working proprietor's most valuable contribution in economic terms. Would it be directly productive operative skill and experience, or an ability to manage people and affairs? Assuming that it is no longer possible to do both, if it is the former then it will be necessary to delegate as many management tasks as possible and may include engaging someone specifically to maintain the books and records. If it is the latter then there will be a need for one extra member of operative staff.

Let us now suppose that you, the reader, are proposing to go into business on your own account and that you are faced with these questions. What would you want to do: Spend most if not all of the time giving your own personal practical service to your clients or concentrate on management? That is something only you can answer.

Why is management necessary?

This question can best be answered by looking at what a manager does, or perhaps more realistically, should do.

While it may be admitted that management is primarily concerned with ensuring productivity and profitability it must never be overlooked that management is also concerned with people, with people as individuals and with people in groups; with human relationships in a commercial context which of necessity implies certain constraints on behaviour. No matter how materially efficient a business may be, if the interpersonal relationships are not satisfactory difficulties of one kind or another are almost bound to arise.

The traditional view of management which regarded managers as people who would *get things done* as opposed to *doing* tended to create a them and us situation which almost inevitably separated the management from the workforce. This may have worked tolerably well in the early days of industrial development when a largely uneducated workforce was often under the control of a better informed management but it is likely to be far less effective in today's climate of universal awareness of employees' rights and entitlements. Consequently modern management thinking has moved towards management in a coordinating role rather than one which merely directs. While there must always be management tasks and responsibilities which differ markedly from those of non-management the tendency to include consultation in management procedures generally leads to a better relationship between management and the workforce.

The exercise of management is thus twofold in nature:

* to promote levels of trading and ensure financial viability;
* to promote suitable interpersonal relationships between all concerned.

While it can be argued that these are of equal importance and interdependent it is obvious that if a business is not productive and profitable it will sooner or later be forced to stop trading regardless of how well the clients, staff and management may get on together.

Clearly, management must be *in control* but this does not give licence to ride roughshod over the legitimate expectations and reasonable feelings of others. When, as was always the case in the past and sometimes in the present, management has absolute power over the workforce then absolute control can be the name of the game but when the balance of power is distributed more or less evenly between the parties concerned a spirit of compromise must come into the relationship if deadlock is to be avoided. Management must be able to recognize the reasonable expectations and legitimate rights of its workforce and the workforce must recognize management's indisputable right to manage in the interests of the business as a whole.

There are many factors which contribute to a truly successful business and any order of listing may be more a matter of convenience than to establish priorities. Below is a slightly more detailed but by no means complete list of the responsibilities of management. Clearly different persons occupying different positions and with different perceived interests in the venture will have their own ideas with regard to priorities:

* productivity and profitability;
* growth and development;
* the business (salon) image;
* customer (client) satisfaction;
* customer (client) welfare and safety;
* interpersonal relationships;
* staff recruitment, training and discipline;
* staff welfare and safety;
* staff incentives and rewards;
* staff career structure and opportunities for advancement.

Management involves both the present and the future. The manager must be capable of handling current situations and able to anticipate future events and plan for future development. This requires a lively mind sensitive to signs which suggest the emergence of new trends, new materials and new methods, and able to identify in advance possible growth areas.

Managers as communicators

As we proceed with our analysis of the role of management one thing will become clear above all others – *managers must be good communicators*. A manager's personal insight and foresight will be of limited value if the relevant message is not communicated effectively to interested or potentially interested parties.

There is, of course, a lot of communication about, but how much of it is truly objective? When you make a statement to another person you are in a misleadingly advantageous position because you know what you mean to convey and your mind will tend to fill in the gaps in the spoken words. Your intended message may seem to be perfectly clear to you but is it equally clear to the other person? To illustrate this point it is only necessary to think back to your schooldays and the occasions when although the teachers apparently knew perfectly well what they were talking about you perhaps quite often did not. It is very likely that much of this lack of understanding may have been your own fault because you were not paying sufficient attention, but how can you be sure that other people will pay proper attention to what you are saying even assuming that you are stating it correctly?

Much of general conversation is more subjective than objective and is often no more than a pleasant and relaxed expression of loosely stated observations, ideas and beliefs. It is not so much a dialogue as a series of monologues because quite often we are too involved in what we want to say to listen properly to anything that could be regarded as a constructive reply. Managers must be able to convey their ideas and messages as clearly and concisely as possible, but equally importantly must be able to listen attentively to the response and be sensitive to its true meaning.

Effective communication is a necessary requirement if we are to deal successfully with our business associates. Communication involves more than technique, it involves an attitude of mind. If you are not convinced about the necessity or usefulness of what you have to say, or lack conviction, you can scarcely hope to convince anyone else. Since what you have to say has an equal chance of not being understood it is important to be quite sure that your message has been accurately conveyed and received. Communication is a two-way process, it involves both giving and receiving information. The manager passes information outwards to staff and customers (clients) and essentially receives responses from those concerned. It is important to bear in mind that these responses may need careful interpretation because they may not necessarily mean what they appear to mean.

Communication may be visual, aural or written, or any combination of these – we see, we hear and most of us can read but the exact nature and significance of a given situation or event is for each of us only what we perceive it to be. Remember also that perceptions can be manipulated. Advertisers using modern media techniques go to a great deal of trouble and expense to persuade us to perceive their own particular products in the image they wish to present.

Communication is not always concerned only with facts, it can, and generally does include ideas, opinions, beliefs, feelings, and emotions, and since most of our supposed judgements are formed within our own minds, although quite often assisted by a little help from outside, it is scarcely possible to make a truly impersonal judgement. Therefore most of our views are coloured by accumulated ideas, opinions and beliefs which are not always our own, together with feelings and emotions which arise from or are aroused within us. We may believe that we both think and act independently but, if we accept a well known psychologist's view that we are primarily stimulus–response mechanisms, this cannot always be true.

Listening

Being on the receiving end of information is not a passive activity. To listen effectively requires concentration and considerable mental effort. Needless to say not many people are very good at it. To listen effectively our minds must be receptive to different interpretations of a given situation, in short, *to other points of view*. We must be prepared to consider interpretations which may be coloured by experiences and emotions different from our own. These differences may stem from different positions in life, from individual personality traits as well as from any of one hundred and one influences which may bear upon us. If our listening is not supported by a genuine desire to understand we may never find out the truth about ourselves and other people.

Staff meetings

Business relationships can benefit from well planned meetings. Such meetings need not necessarily be long or frequent and under normal circumstances even as little as two or three times a year may be sufficient. Unnecessary meetings with an ill-defined agenda lose their impact and even become positively boring and an apparent waste of time to those present. Clearly there must be a definite reason for calling any meeting and equally that meeting must be well planned beforehand. Management must know clearly what needs to be said but at the same time must be prepared to encourage comment and enter into reasonable discussion. No one person is possessed of all the good ideas. If the management is not prepared to listen to staff and give full and unbiased consideration to genuine suggestions then some good ideas may be lost and employees may be discouraged from taking a proper interest and pride in their place of work. Obviously some ideas may be unworkable simply because members of staff do not have access to all of the facts known to the management. Nevertheless, such suggestions should not be bluntly dismissed out of hand with possible discomfiture for the proposer which may well have the effect of silencing that particular individual at all future meetings.

In large organizations where top management is removed from the work environment at shopfloor (salon) level it is vitally important to listen to the views of middle management or senior members of staff who may have a better knowledge of the problems arising out of the actual work situation and a better insight into possible causes and probable solutions.

Reasons for meetings

Obviously there can be many reasons for calling a staff meeting depending on circumstances prevailing at any given time. In more general terms a meeting may be called to:

* give necessary information;
* receive necessary information;
* test existing attitudes and feelings;
* secure desirable attitudes;
* resolve a particular problem.

For example, a meeting may be necessary when it is proposed to:

* make positive changes in working methods;
* introduce new services;
* introduce updated equipment;
* promote retail products;
* discontinue an unprofitable service or product;
* increase staffing;
* extend staff training.

Finally, all meetings should be totally objective and preferably as concise as possible. Social relaxation comes at the end of the meeting, or if it is likely to be a long one then with a break in the middle. At no time should any item be allowed to imply criticism of a particular member of staff, or for that matter extravagant praise which might lead to thoughts of favouritism. Such matters should always be dealt with in privacy between management and the person concerned.

5 The staff

The most valuable asset a hairdressing or beauty therapy business can possess is undoubtedly its workforce, especially the operative staff who are the direct producers of salon revenue. Here the stock-in-trade is not goods but the technical, artistic and social skills of those who carry out the various processes. Other members of staff also have an important contribution to make to overall efficiency and a high level of productivity.

Premises, furnishings, decor and equipment can do much to ensure a physical salon environment which is both attractive and comfortable. In addition to such material matters, however, a salon can acquire what we may call *an atmosphere*; a distinct, perhaps even unique, personality which sets it apart from all others and which is the sum total of the personalities of the management and all who work in that salon. This corporate personality may occur naturally but is more likely to be the result of management policy and careful selection and training of the workforce. Many business organizations quite often spend a great deal of time and money in attempting to bring together a workforce which can meet their criteria of excellence in providing their particular service or services to the public.

Ideally the salon staff should present the image of a harmonious whole, working with the sole aim of giving satisfaction to the clientele. This does not mean, however, that they must be alike in their individual personalities. Indeed if we can use the simile of a group of people singing in unison with the different voices all taking the same notes this can be somewhat dull and uninteresting, but if that same group is capable of singing in harmony with the different voices taking different parts and complementing each other to produce a balanced whole then we have a sound which is a delight to the discriminating ear. So it can be with staff who may individually be quite different in personality but are capable of working together in harmony. This is particularly desirable in hairdressing and beauty therapy salons where staff are frequently working side by side under the watchful eye of the clientele. To achieve such teamwork involves choosing people who can not only provide their own individual contribution to the various services but are capable of working happily in harmony with others to present an overall image which will attract and hold custom in the immediate vicinity and beyond.

It is never good policy to engage new staff in a hurry. Time taken in selection and in ensuring as far as possible that the new member(s) will harmonize with the existing staff may avoid some headaches later on. Personal service businesses need permanent staff who will get to know and identify satisfactorily with other employees and the clients. Frequent staff changes are almost always a bad sign and suggest that there may be something wrong with the place of work, its atmosphere, management and/or employee relationships, pay and/or career prospects, or just inefficient selection of staff.

Interviewing and selection

Preferably before advertising a post and certainly before interviewing it is helpful to prepare a job description or personnel specification. This is in fact a pen picture of the ideal person for the job and identifies the immediate and potential skills and personal qualities you are looking for.

Some people who interview impressively may not live up to this early promise and so it is the potential of the proposed new employee which is most important, which includes how well they will fit into the existing team together with a willingness to learn additional skills and to adapt to perhaps different methods and procedures. Past experience is of great importance but inevitably there will be some need to adjust to a new environment and possibly new situations as they arise.

While immediate financial reward is important, a lively and capable would-be employee may also want to be assured that there will be an adequate career structure with opportunities for further training and future development.

Since all applicants will normally be interviewed it is worthwhile to consider in advance how the interview should proceed. Remember that ideally an interview is a two-way affair. You, as the prospective employer, will want to find out if the applicant is suitable for the job and equally the applicant will want to find out what the job involves in terms of work, pay and conditions.

It is most important that the applicant should feel at ease and able to speak freely. There should be no interruptions which could break the continuity of the interview. The interviewer's questions should encourage explanations or more extended answers rather than just plain yes or no. The purpose is to draw out the applicant and encourage frankness and freedom of speech. Bear in mind that *it is what the applicant actually has to say which can be most revealing.* If the interviewer dominates the situation and talks too much many applicants, particularly the young and inexperienced, will withdraw into themselves and say very little of real significance.

In cases where the job requires a satisfactory level of existing practical skill and experience it is not unusual to include a demonstration of ability by asking the applicant to carry out certain tasks. This need not be on the day of the interview but on a subsequent day when it could be limited to the most likely applicants. All applicants should, of course, be advised well before the date of the interview that this may be required.

Staff training and development

Staff training involves more than merely providing the opportunity to pursue a college course or attend manufacturers' trade schools, although these can make a very valuable contribution. In general, college courses are most useful in offering supplementary training to junior staff to enable them to gain appropriate City and Guilds and other qualifications and to prepare senior staff for the more advanced examinations. Manufacturers' trade schools play an important part in respect of instruction in the proper use of their specialized equipment and products and in many of the currently fashionable techniques for which they are largely responsible. Nevertheless, it is an inescapable fact that the first priority of the average commercial salon is to train its staff essentially to meet the needs and wants of their own particular clientele and that they will tend to view staff training in that context.

Motivation is an important aspect of in-salon staff training. Staff will need to feel that the time and effort given to extending their skill and experience to meet the needs of that particular salon will be suitably rewarded in terms of financial benefit and/or job satisfaction.

It is well known that many people tend to work harder when

there is a financial reward at the end. In monotonous and fatiguing tasks the provision of such a reward is often found to be the only way to support effort and energy expenditure and raise standards of performance. Rewards can, however, be of many kinds ranging from mere money to the personal satisfaction of a job well done. Perhaps one of the least common and yet the most effective of all motivators is achievement motivation or the satisfaction derived from the elegant performance of a skilled act for its own sake.

Exactly what it is that motivates and supports particular patterns of behaviour in individuals is often difficult to define and yet it is clear that under normal circumstances the hairdresser and the beauty therapist will seek and enjoy the approval of their clients. Thus it is inevitable that the individual operative will attract a personal clientele and that between them will exist a state of empathy. Such personal clientele will often be attracted for reasons other than the level of technical and/or artistic skill exhibited by the operative and will hold that operative's work in high esteem in a mutually satisfactory personal relationship. It is worthy of consideration that the satisfaction of performing familiar tasks in a warm and friendly atmosphere with the evident approval of a personal clientele may afford motivation for the average hairdresser or beauty therapist which is at least equal to financial gain or the acquisition of a high standard of technical and/or artistic ability. Indeed it is evident that many hairdressers, for example, with no more than adequate skill in the management of hair but who have a natural aptitude for pleasing and managing people are frequently the most successful commercially.

Cooperative elements

It is considered that people motivate each other when they perform cooperatively together; that they derive benefit from the greater amount of resource input available. The busy hairdressing salon, for example, has a high level of general activity which when well organized undoubtedly has a motivating effect upon the majority of those so engaged, for although they may not be actually performing together in a single task there is a sharing of overall effort to cope with the workload. Not all individuals, however, cooperate equally effectively and some are at their best when they are *doing their own thing*.

Competitive elements

Competitive urges are clearly a basic component of the human personality, although it is evident that some people respond more to this form of motivation than others. Before competition can take place the individuals must perceive themselves to be in a competitive situation. The presence of two individuals working side by side on similar tasks does not necessarily imply a competitive state. Whereas some people see almost every aspect of human endeavour in competitive terms others may be barely conscious of this except when it is made particularly obvious by the behaviour of their associates.

There are many occasions when a competitive environment can motivate the participants to attempt to achieve a superior performance but there is always the ever-present danger that an excess of competitiveness may adversely affect personal relationships to an extent that will preclude cooperative working and damage environmental harmony. Clearly this raises the question of whether a profit-sharing scheme is a better inducement to cooperative working as opposed to the more competitive system of individual commission.

6 The clients

Many thousands of women of all ages and from all walks of life avail themselves of the services provided by the hairdresser and to a lesser extent the services of the beauty therapist. Some on a regular, at least weekly, basis and others intermittently for some particular attention when required.

Clearly women attend the salon primarily for the services they need, or want, but there is also one important aspect of the visit that must never be overlooked – they will generally expect to enjoy the experience and go away personally satisfied with the result.

Much of the day-to-day life of the average hairdresser and beauty therapist is spent in pleasing or trying to please people; people of many different types and personalities and often with widely differing expectations both with regard to the final outcome and the manner in which they would like to be treated during the process. The majority of women have a strong sense of social affiliation, infinitely more so than most men. It is important for a woman to feel that she is liked and to like those she deals with. It is also important that the salon environment should be attractive, comfortable and caring. Almost all women enjoy the luxury of personal attention in a congenial atmosphere.

The highest standard of hygiene together with general tidiness is essential. There will be those who do not particularly notice such things but there will always be a sufficient number who do and who will fully appreciate an apparent recognition of their own personal sensitivity.

The overall image of the salon is of great significance but beware of indulging your own personal tastes and even prejudices in a way that could be unattractive to many of your existing or potential clients. A little consumer research to determine the nature of local custom and the possibility of encouraging other custom from further afield could be well worth the time and effort taken.

It is necessary to accept that we cannot hope to please all of the people. Clients will come and they will either stay or they will go. Exactly what it was that kept one and drove another away is often difficult to determine. The majority of people would not reveal what it was that did not please them even supposing they actually knew. It could easily have been some small thing that might have appeared irrelevant to you had you even been aware of it. There will be others who will readily complain in no uncertain terms and the curious thing is that in spite of their grumbles many of them will often become permanent customers, perhaps in some cases when you would rather be without them.

It is not easy to cater for people of all types and age groups, and often very different tastes and expectations. Television viewers must be aware that this media, especially where it is sponsored by advertising, aims its programmes at a majority audience which often leaves the minority taste somewhat out in the cold. In the field of hairdressing it is possible that some of the more conventional people, especially some of the older ones, would not be comfortable in a salon catering exclusively for the young and trendy while on the other hand many of the young people would perhaps prefer a currently fashionable unisex salon to the more conventional establishment. There are, however, many salons which do succeed in catering for a wide range of people and they do this mainly by avoiding the extremes in their image. Beware you do not make drastic unconsidered changes in your salon environment which could discourage and eventually lose altogether a minority group of otherwise loyal and financially important clients. Many people appreciate a salon where they can exchange the stresses and strains of everyday life, including the high level of background noise we now suffer, for a pleasant chat or a quiet read while they are being pampered just a little.

It is not always a good policy to blindly follow a trend just because it appears to be the in thing. Sometimes we can make a greater impact by remaining more or less as we are even if that means no more than being quiet and attentive while offering services of high quality. If you are considering the introduction of something new and quite different into the salon environment which leaves the unappreciative client no choice but to accept it or go elsewhere it would be well worthwhile to check beforehand on possible reactions. Time spent in identifying the clients which you, your particular expertise and working environment have the best chance of pleasing is never a waste of effort. The first aim is to attract those clients, the second aim is to please them, while the last and even more difficult aim is to keep them.

It could prove to be a useful and perhaps revealing exercise to ask as many people as possible of different types, age groups and walks of life the following question:

What particular aspects of social, environmental and practical service in a salon would displease you and deter you from returning?

Ask them to say whatever immediately comes to mind, followed by more considered replies and be sure to write everything down at once. Try to arrange the replies in an order of priority from the most to the least intolerable. It may serve to uncover some things that may have been happening in your salon apparently unnoticed by your staff or, for that matter, yourself.

7 Social skills

Social skills could be simply defined as the art of managing people by putting them at their ease, making them feel that they are liked and appreciated and that their personal feelings and wishes are receiving due consideration. But as with most things in life it is not quite as simple as that, for it can truly be said that *everything in this world is no more and no less than we individually perceive it to be.*

Therefore we must not fall into the trap of believing that our own perception of any given situation is necessarily the same for other people. At least some of them will have a quite different view, different sensitivity and different personal tastes. It is therefore essential that the would-be successful hairdresser or beauty therapist should recognize this inescapable fact from the outset. It is not, of course, possible to be truly all things to all people but it is possible to acquire a professional manner which will achieve a balance between formality and informality and leave us personally uninvolved. Perhaps the most outstanding example of this is in the case of a nurse who, if she is to survive, needs a caring attitude with a minimum of emotional involvement.

The social skills of service

Fortunately quite a lot of people are not too demanding and not too difficult to please but there are always the others who have precise expectations of any situation and will not hesitate to make their displeasure known if those expectations are not met. Even so, all but a very few can be won over by the right approach and subsequent careful management. The only question of importance is whether you can live with or without them as clients? There is always the chance that if you do please such a person she may well become one of your most devoted clients mainly because you have taken the trouble to succeed where others have failed. The satisfied client may or may not tell her friends how good you are but the dissatisfied client is quite likely to broadcast her discontent and that would not be at all good for business.

It is important to categorize the range of skills necessary for a successful hairdresser or beauty therapist. In any musical or visual art performance absolute command of the chosen instrument or media is a necessary prerequisite to sensitive interpretation and presentation. In hairdressing and beauty therapy adequate technical skill is the first essential. This can then be supported and presented with the aid of suitable social skills to emerge as a completely acceptable service. What then are the social skills which are so desirable? There is, of course, more to it than the somewhat oversimplified definition provided by one hairdressing student, who said: 'If you chat them up enough you can get away with anything'. Even so, he had a point, albeit expressed in rough and ready language.

Let us now consider in slightly more detail the client's possible social contacts from the moment of entering the salon to the moment of leaving it.

The first contact will be by making an enquiry and/or booking an appointment. Clearly the response to an initial enquiry and the image presented at that time must be satisfactory or the appointment may not be booked. The answer to the enquiry must convince the potential client that she can reasonably expect to get the service she wants and the image presented must be one of efficiency and enthusiasm.

If the enquiry is by telephone then the total image will be an aural one. Therefore, tone of voice, manner of speaking and clarity of information are paramount. The conclusion of the conversation is also important and should convey that the enquiry and the subsequent booking are welcome and appreciated. In the interests of efficiency and to avoid later misunderstanding it is always helpful to repeat the day and time of the appointment and the service booked at the end of the conversation in order to fix it firmly in the client's mind.

Enquiry and/or booking in person at reception also involves tone of voice, manner of speaking and clarity of information but because it is also visual it poses other problems which include the appearance and deportment of the receptionist and the image presented by other members of staff who may be in reception at that time, together with decor, tidiness and comfort of the reception area and finally that indefinable thing known as social atmosphere.

When any client or potential client enters reception she should receive immediate attention or at least recognition of her presence. If receptionist is occupied with another client at that moment, a smile in the client's direction together with a 'good morning/afternoon, I will not keep you long' will make her feel noticed and welcome. No one enjoys being ignored even for a short time.

A client should never wait in reception for her appointment a moment longer than is absolutely necessary and when this is unavoidable she should be made as comfortable as possible and kept informed of the position. Never let frustration at being kept waiting build up. Attention at intervals during waiting will help to dissipate tension.

A client's progress through the various processes in the salon should be comfortable and supported by an evident desire on the part of staff for her well-being and satisfaction.

It is important that staff should be sensitive to differences in temperament between one client and another. Some like to relax and be quiet while the operative gets on with whatever needs to be done while others of a more lively disposition like to converse on a variety of subjects. Operatives should avoid the temptation to air their own views too strongly and should learn the value of listening: showing interest, sympathy and understanding with whatever the client wishes to say, even if the subject matter happens to be one they, personally, do not find particularly interesting.

Many women come to regard their hairdresser or beauty therapist as a friend and confidant and under the relaxing influence of treatment will sometimes talk about their personal problems. *Respect that confidence at all times and never ever repeat what you have been told.*

Each client should feel that her personal custom is valued and that she is a necessary part of your business life. It cannot be repeated too often that the name of the game is *pleasing people*. With a few notable exceptions the business life of a hairdresser or beauty therapist comprises just that. Always remember that the client does not simply buy a permanent wave or a beauty treatment but a complete service which must be totally satisfying to that client. No matter how well you may think you have done, if the client is not pleased then in business terms you have in that instance failed.

Even when the service is satisfactorily completed and the client is happy with the result all is not yet over because she still has to pass once more through reception and departure must be just as carefully managed as arrival. Service must continue until the moment the client makes her exit through the door which has been thoughtfully opened for her by the receptionist. The receptionist should know exactly what has been done for the client and should offer a suitable comment of approval with the result. After all, if the client has just spent quite a bit of money on a service intended to improve her appearance she will appreciate the effect being noticed.

It makes a useful exercise to construct a progress chart for a particular service, following the client through from booking and arrival to ultimate departure and note at each stage the kinds of social skills which can and should be applied. Having drawn up this ideal plan it can then be compared with what actually goes on in reception and the salon during a normal day. Observe different clients receiving different services with different members of staff and note those instances which are nearest to the ideal and those which are farthest from it. Consider carefully how the social environment and the standards of comfort and service could be improved.

The social skills of management

Staff

While the social skills of service generally involve a two-part relationship between operative and client, effective management involves a somewhat more complex relationship between three parties comprising operative, client and manager. The expectations of both client and operative need to be met and management must function effectively in the best interests of the business as a whole.

It has been said that 'instrumental authority is incompatible with universal popularity' and there is some truth in that statement if only because of the almost inevitable conflict between perceived interests in any situation. Note the use of the word 'perceived' interests because we do not necessarily always know precisely where our best interests lie. Clearly the public image and prosperity of a business brings profits to the owners but it also ensures continuing employment for a competent workforce. Yet in spite of this apparently obvious fact workers sometimes adopt attitudes and take courses of action which appear to attack the very fabric of the organization which employs them.

A business can be managed in a number of ways from uncompromising authority to the other extreme of a loosely democratic or even laissez-faire attitude. What is required is a balance between an authoritative and a democratic approach.

Many people like to feel that they are being consulted but quite often this is rather more a matter of status than a strong desire to become deeply involved in the responsibility of decision making. To complain is a common human practice but to be able to offer a realistic solution to a particular difficulty which will take into account the interests of all parties is quite another matter.

It is important to keep staff in the picture with regard to developments which may affect their own perceived interests but clearly there will be a limit to the amount and type of information which can be divulged to everybody. However, for the most part employees do like to know where they stand; what they can and cannot do, what they can expect from the employer and what the employer will expect from them.

All personal relationships in business need to achieve a reasonable balance between the formal and the informal. Friendliness without familiarity is the essential formulae which applies equally to all parties. It all comes down once more to that indefinable thing called atmosphere. Once the right atmosphere has been established in terms of relationships in a business and no sense of injustice has been allowed to develop then there should not be too many problems between management and staff which cannot be solved through discussion and negotiation.

If management is seen to be obviously caring as well as reasonably authoritative most employees will accept the status quo. Management which is demonstrably both supportive and effective in terms of the business and all of those engaged in its activities must inevitably at least earn respect. The best organizations adopt a paternal attitude with real concern for the happiness and well-being of the workforce. This does not mean indulgence but a fair bargain where skill and effort is rewarded and human needs and aspirations are fully recognized. It is important for employees to feel that they are truly valued and are personally making a meaningful contribution to the image and prosperity of the business – *a pride in the work and in the place of work*.

At all times be sincere, be just, and treat all employees with proper consideration. Never make hasty judgements about individual behaviour. There is always a cause for any behaviour pattern if only you can find out what it is. Until you can identify that cause you have little chance of finding a remedy and a way of keeping someone who in different circumstances may be a satisfactory member of staff.

It is important to be able to recognize:

* areas of activity where management can and must exercise authority in the best interests of the business;
* where consultation with employees would be desirable or essential in the interests of good relationships;
* possible areas of conflict of interests between management and employees, and how undesirable situations could be avoided or resolved;
* possible areas of conflict of interests between one employee and another and how undesirable situations could be avoided or resolved;
* early warning signs of dissatisfaction of one kind or another.

Clients

There is one fundamental practical difference forming the basis of the relationship between management and clients as opposed to the relationship between management and staff. Quite simply, the *clients are paying to receive a service* whereas the *staff are being paid to give a service*. This does not mean that the staff should be treated any less fairly than the clients but it does mean that the clients may have the advantage should a situation arise where it becomes a question of choice between the interests of one or the other. Ideally, the need for such a decision should not arise too often if the management has acquired a happy, loyal and dedicated staff which recognizes that their personal income as well as that of the business depends upon a satisfied clientele.

Some clients may not be particularly sensitive to atmosphere but there are others who will quickly detect any sign of conflict between management and staff. While it is essential that management should be seen to be in control, many clients will be disturbed if that control seems to be too strongly assertive and unreasonable to the evident discomfiture of a member of staff whom they may look upon with favour. The result of such a situation could well be to strengthen that interpersonal relationship, damage the influence of management and undermine confidence in its fairness and efficiency. Insensitive management can easily disturb the balance of relationships within a business and may even drive some clients away. Management which demonstrates confidence and trust in the staff must also inspire the confidence of the clientele.

It is almost inevitable in the case of a large business that top management will become detached from the clientele but management at local level or senior staff can still maintain a valuable personal relationship. This problem is not so likely to arise where the manager not only manages but also attends personally to some of the clients.

The manager should always show a personal interest in the work of the staff and never forget to include the member of staff in any discussion regarding the requirements of the client. Hairdressing and beauty therapy are personal services provided in a personal environment, therefore the ideal to aim at is a happy working family atmosphere where everyone is working together to give satisfactory service.

Sometimes the manager may need to reprimand a member of staff for some misdemeanour, for an incorrect attitude towards a client or for obvious neglect of a client. *This should never be done in the presence of the client* because it could prove to be extremely embarrassing to both client and member of staff and would almost certainly create an unfavourable image of relationships in general. There is an old saying which advises never to wash your dirty linen in public and the modern open salon is a very public place. Correction of any kind should always be made in private away from clients and other members of staff if they are not directly involved in the incident.

Clients attend a hairdressing or beauty therapy salon for the primary purpose of receiving a practical service but quite reasonably they also expect to enjoy the experience. This can sometimes make great demands upon the management, particularly in the case of a large and busy salon, to ensure that everything goes smoothly and satisfactorily from the moment of entry to the moment of departure.

It is important to be able to recognize:

* possible expectations of clients of different types and from different walks of life, and how management could achieve a balanced social environment which would be pleasing to a varied clientele;
* the kinds of attention some clients might expect from the management over and above that provided by the operative staff;
* possible areas of clients' dissatisfaction with management;
* possible differences in the perceived interests of clients, operatives and management and how to avoid or resolve undesirable conflict between these interests.

8 Advertising

Modern advertising as practised by the experts is rarely just a matter of letting the public know that a product or service exists. Most advertising has quite precise aims and it has strategies. Advertising should have:

* a clear objective in terms of what it is expected to do;
* a target group in terms of the particular people it is intended to influence;
* at least an implied benefit for the consumer and an image of what that benefit is in terms of the particular target group;
* reasons why the consumer should choose that particular product or service rather than any other.

With regard to benefit it is an interesting exercise to list the main characteristics of a particular product or service, such as a motor car, living accommodation or a holiday and ask a random group of people to place those characteristics in their own personal order of priority. It is a fair bet that for each of them number one on their own list will have a strong personal advertising appeal.

It is important to 'position' a particular service or product in a way which will be attractive to the target group. Position can be defined as 'the place held by a person or thing' and so when you position a particular hairdressing or beauty service you place it in a certain way in the potential client's mind. For example, when promoting a hair colouring service for the middle-aged woman you could say:

Glamorcolor is the most effective way of covering unwanted grey hair!

or

Glamorcolor hides nature's imperfections and makes you look even younger!

The first example ends on a somewhat depressing note and limits its benefit to the not very exciting prospect of merely covering grey hair, whereas the second leaves the client to privately place her own interpretation on the relevant imperfection (in this case grey hair) and ends on a buoyant note by suggesting that she can look even younger. Not merely younger but *even younger* which adds just a subtle touch of flattery.

It is generally a question of identifying a weakness in the defences of the particular target group, what that group will see as a benefit and why they should patronize your business rather than any other. Clearly what may be seen as a benefit by one group may have very little appeal for another group for a variety of reasons. A type of holiday which would attract a group of lively teenagers going away together would hardly prove suitable for a young married couple with several small children, and an elderly couple would almost certainly need something different again. Think about target groups and ask yourself the question 'who am I trying to influence and how best can I do it'.

Copywriting

Newspaper reporters frequently use a technique which is known as 'slamming up the headlines'. It is really quite easy to do. For example, the headline 'Dog bites man' would hardly merit more than a passing glance but if this can be given dramatic or emotive overtones it will inevitably attract more attention, and so it becomes 'Savage Alsatian attacks unemployed father of three'. It is, of course, desirable that the statement should be in essence true but this is sometimes not strictly the case.

The purpose of a newspaper headline is twofold

* To encourage people to buy the paper.
  and
* To encourage a desire to read on and find out more about it.

It will make an interesting exercise to

* Select a newspaper item with an emotive, dramatic or startling headline and then read the text which follows to see if it really justifies such a headline.
  or
* First cover up such a headline and ask a group of people who have not previously seen it to read the text and

suggest their own headline. They may be surprised to find how tame some of their own headlines are compared with the original.

or

* Write a simple factual report of some incident which may have occurred and ask the group to suggest slammed up headlines.

It is essential that copy for an advertisement should be constructed in such a way that it will encourage the potential client to read on or to call and find out more about it. It is also essential that the client should see that there could be a benefit in it for her, but be careful not to make or positively imply any promise about a particular service which cannot be supported by the result otherwise you may offend against the Trade Descriptions Acts of 1968–72.

Sometimes copywriters and/or illustrators are quite clever at creating situations where the reader, or in particular the viewer, makes assumptions about things which are not directly stated. In such cases it could be difficult to prove there was any intention to mislead even though we may know in our own minds that this must have been so.

Advertisements often make subjective claims which cannot be tested. To advertise 'an Apple pie like mother used to make' really promises nothing because although some mothers must have made very good apple pies there would have been others who made apple pies that were pretty awful and, in any event, it makes no claim for the excellence of the pie, only that it is like mother used to make. Those whose mothers made good apple pies will make the connection and probably buy one. In our earlier example, to say that 'Glamorcolor . . . makes you look even younger' cannot be tested because in order to do so we need to know 'younger than what or whom?'. A washing powder that claims to wash whiter raises the question 'whiter than what?'.

It is only when an objective claim or a direct promise is made that problems begin to arise and the advertiser can really be challenged to show that what has been said is substantially true.

All people do not necessarily see things in the same way and what may appear attractive to one person may be uninteresting or even offensive to another. Therefore when you set out to create an image for your particular salon do not expect everyone to be equally impressed.

It is important to distinguish between advertising for short-term effect such as a special product promotion or a currently

popular fashion trend and long-term effect such as consolidat-
ing the overall positioning of the business. It is an advantage to
be an individual, setting yourself slightly apart as something
special, provided that does not mean ignoring the sensibilities
of some people you might want as clients. Even so, it is better
to avoid positioning that is exactly the same as your competitors. Indeed you may be substantially the same but nevertheless able to build into your image that something which
suggests you are a little bit different.

It is important to decide which aspect of what you have to
offer is likely to appeal to a given target group, bearing in mind
that you can change the target group from time to time by
advertising, for example, something that will appeal to the
teenage population one week and something that will appeal
to the older woman a week or so later. Never try to do both
things at once because one may have a negative effect on the
other.

Remember that times and attitudes change – sometimes the
market will respond and sometimes it will not. Be careful your
innovative advertising is not too early or too late, for what was
in fashion yesterday may be out of fashion today, and who
knows about tomorrow? Think how many pop groups reach
the top, then fall out of favour and are never heard of again.

Remember also that forward positioning is the key to long-
term success if you want your business to continue to prosper.
You may be determined to follow your own inclinations and
present a current image that appeals particularly to you but
bear in mind that you are not a client and that many potential
clients may have quite different needs and expectations both
now and in the future. If you go exclusively for high fashion
then you may be limiting your market and discouraging a
significant number of people who have ignored extremes of
fashion for most of their lives and will probably continue to do
so. Always think carefully before embarking on a programme
which excludes good alternative sources of revenue. In a
recent management examination one candidate wrote that she
would include only two hood dryers in her design for a salon
because she would want to discourage such old-fashioned
services as perms and shampoos and sets and concentrate on
exotic hair colouring for young people. Hairdressers and
beauty therapists are, or should be, primarily in business to
provide a range of services that the public at large both needs
and wants. Think what happens to areas dependent upon a
single industry such as cotton, coal mining or ship building
when the demand for the products of those industries
declines.

The unisex salon

You may be offering services exclusively for women or for both men and women. Do not make the mistake of assuming that because both men and women may attend the same places that they necessarily view things in the same way. The unisex idea may work well in certain circumstances but there are fundamental differences of attitude between the sexes and they generally have different personal expectations. Never be patronizing about sex, age or taste.

Try writing an advertisement which might appeal equally to men and women and you will soon appreciate the difficulty. If you own a unisex salon then write an advertisement which is designed to appeal to women one week and an advertisement which is designed to appeal to men a week or so later.

The picture that tells a story

The use of photographs in advertising can be an expensive proposition but it is worth remembering the news editor's old saying 'a good photograph is worth several hundred words of copy'. Teachers and lecturers know the value of visual aids and frequently use them to get across the desired message.

Most people respond to visual images, hence the enormous popularity of television. Visual perception develops much sooner than aural perception and after that we have to learn to read. Many small children who cannot yet read and who would be unable to follow anything but the simplest stories on sound radio will often watch television with great interest. The great attraction of the animated cartoon rests in the movement of figures on ground. There does not have to be and rarely is a storyline of any significance – it is the movement or action which counts. It probably all goes back to our animal ancestry when anything that moved immediately attracted attention if only to give early man time to avoid becoming a meal for that approaching carnivore.

A single still picture in a press advertisement or in your salon window cannot generally tell the whole story but if it has the right impact it will attract the attention of the reader or the passer-by. Sometimes an interesting item of new equipment can have a similar effect and many years ago when the first so-called 'wireless' system of permanent waving came onto the market, which really meant the client was no longer uncomfortably attached to a machine by wires, the author featured the Callinan system (an impressive piece of equipment which looked a bit like a communications satellite) in a salon window display where it attracted a great deal of attention for many weeks and resulted in much new business. It was at its most impressive when suitably floodlit in the evenings. Remember it is the impact which counts. It must stop the potential clients in their tracks and draw them to the window to find out more about it.

There is a currently popular technique used largely in television media advertising which sets up an action sequence designed to attract attention without appearing to have any connection with any product. It is not until the sequence ends that the advertising message appears. Perhaps viewers have now become so accustomed to the normal rather bland advertisements that they tend to ignore them and this is an attempt to stimulate interest before delivering the punchline.

However what may work in visual action advertising cannot be readily applied to static media. Therefore a picture which does not identify with the text of a printed advertisement could hinder rather than help the message you are trying to get across. Sometimes a picture can lead into text which is designed to add detail to a visual message and sometimes it can be used to illustrate a headline statement. It is important to be quite clear about what the picture is actually intended to do and to make sure it is the right picture for the purpose. It is useful to ask yourself such questions as:

* Is the picture meant to create the first impact and exactly what message is the picture meant to convey?
* Does the text pick up that message and extend it into further explanation?
* Is the picture meant to give support to a leading statement and does it do this effectively?

Not everyone is photogenic and a featured hairstyle, for example, must be on the right person and – equally important – photographed from exactly the right angle. That attractive model pictured in a fashion magazine was not the result of just one take but probably ten, twenty or even thirty attempts to capture just the right image.

Cost effectiveness

It is important to be able to make an advance estimate of the probable cost effectiveness of any particular advertising media it is proposed to use and perhaps even more important to make a post-advertising assessment of the results in order to judge its value for future use.

It is self-evident that much of the advertising media used by large companies and organizations with nationwide outlets would be quite unsuitable for a small business with purely local interests. Thus television, radio (other than perhaps local radio), the national press and magazines with a country-wide distribution could not possibly give a return which would justify the very large cost involved.

It is hardly necessary to point out that cost of advertising which is not eventually recovered through revenue from increased trading simply adds another overhead expense to be met out of normal takings. Any manufacturer marketing a new product will have carefully calculated recovery of marketing costs and will know exactly when a break-even point should be reached indicating that recovery has been achieved. There would be no financial benefit in marketing a product where the marketing costs cancelled out the profits. It is only when it is a purely image building or goodwill exercise that this would be allowed to happen.

Advertising is a business expense which must be met out of revenue and only when the cost has been recovered from additional revenue generated will extra profit be made. Sometimes it is necessary to advertise simply to maintain the existing position of the business in the eyes of the public. In this case it can be not so much a question of *can you afford to advertise* but rather one of *can you afford NOT to advertise*, particularly when your main competitors are doing so with good effect.

Ultimately a decision has to be made about what is best for the long-term good of the business, but remember that a great deal of advertising is for the most part transitory – it is effective only for so long as it remains in the eye or in the mind. That is why large impersonal companies marketing nationwide products can never stop or even slow down their advertising.

Money spent on advertising is not the same thing as money ploughed back into the business in the form of fixed assets that will be productive for a long time to come. If you have to choose between a costly advertising campaign and installing much needed new and/or improved equipment in your salon it could be that the equipment will be the better investment in the long run.

Manufacturers go to considerable trouble to find out why people buy their products and how they came to know about them; was it from the recommendation of a friend, as a result of press advertising and in which publication, or was it as a result of television advertising? You may spend money on advertising but that does not necessarily mean all new custom came as a result of that publicity. Perhaps it was through recommendation, your attractive window display, or even as a result of your competitive charges. It is always useful to know how they got to know about you and exactly what it was that attracted them to your salon rather than some other – it could help to determine your approach to publicity in the future.

Press advertising

Classified advertisements provide the cheapest form of press advertising but they are often ignored by those who are not particularly looking for something – they simply turn over those pages. Classified advertisements, particularly when there are very many, can be tedious to read and it is only the idly curious with time to spare or those looking for something specific who are likely to bother. Equally, small display advertisements can be passed over except by those whose attention is caught and who choose to let themselves become involved. Therefore display advertisements must be presented to signal to those – perhaps only a minority of the readers – who represent the target group, and the headlines must be aimed to encourage them to read on.

Sometimes when an advertisement seems not to be having the desired effect a carefully considered change of copy may do the trick. It is not always possible to say why a particular tactic works – we know when it works by the results but not always why or how. We learn from actual experience what best serves a particular purpose in respect of a given individual or group.

An advertisement in a local free newspaper with an average circulation of 75 000 per issue suggests that it will be seen by at least that many people but:

* How many actually read the paper from cover to cover?
* How many are in the target group which may respond to your particular advertisement?
* How many in that target group might find it too inconvenient or too expensive to travel specially to your salon?

Such papers sometimes produce a purely local edition and others produce separate editions or combine a number of localities together in the one edition. Some of these papers will contain advertisements from businesses as far as ten or twenty miles away but they are usually offering products or services which are used only occasionally. It must be borne in mind that hairdressing and beauty therapy services may be required once or even twice a month and sometimes every week. Not many people would find it convenient to make a round trip of twenty to forty miles that frequently when they may be able to obtain an equally satisfactory service in their own locality.

Leaflets

Door to door distribution of leaflets will generally be truly local. However, since it is scarcely possible to know very much about the people to whom such leaflets are distributed it is very likely that many of them will fall on stony ground. If the production and distribution of leaflets costs say £40 and results in only ten new clients then the publicity will have cost £4 per new client. If they continue to patronize your salon and become permanent clients then the exercise will have been worthwhile, but if they attend once only then a one-off cost of £4 must be set against profits in each case and may not have been worth the exercise.

Leaflets available through reception in the salon will cost no more than the price of printing but since that would be to some extent preaching to the converted they have to offer more than general information about services already familiar to existing clients. Quite an effective way is to produce leaflets which offer a benefit to the existing client for each new client introduced. This could be in the form of a free conditioning treatment, a temporary colouring treatment, or a manicure, and even more generous offers could be made where appropriate. Many large business organizations have been doing this kind of thing for many years and it is now spreading into hitherto unlikely activities such as insurance and banking.

There are many ways of promoting trade and no doubt new ideas will continue to arrive as competition for custom increases.

The 'baker's dozen' is a very old but still effective selling tactic in which the customer gets thirteen for the price of twelve. You could offer a free blow-dry or a free manicure as a thirteenth service at the end of twelve provided the twelve services are taken up within a specified time. In one year this could prove to be a worthwhile saving to the client on the cost of regular attention. If your business could afford it and you are feeling generous this could be as often as one in six or one in eight.

Special offers

Special offers are not so readily applicable to services as they are to products. Hairdressers and beauty therapists do not have surplus services to sell off at a small profit or at a break-even price. Special offers for a limited period may be useful in introducing a new service you wish to promote but in general terms they should be regarded as a last resort when it is necessary to cover cost of labour and overheads in order to get over a particularly slack period and keep staff employed.

Demonstrations and exhibitions

Putting on a demonstration or an exhibition can be both expensive and hard work, sometimes with few obvious benefits at the end of it all. It can prove to be a morale boosting success or an utter flop. When considering such a venture it is necessary to ask yourself the following questions

* Are the general public likely to attend, say, a hairdressing demonstration in sufficient numbers to make it really worthwhile?
* Can you afford the level of publicity which will be absolutely essential before the event takes place?
* What will be the scale of the demonstration, where can it be held and how much will it cost?
* Will your staff be happy to take part and will they be able to present their work with flair and confidence? Remember it is one thing to exercise skills in the relative security of a familiar place, the salon, and quite another to expose those skills to the possibly critical gaze of a large audience in a public place.
* Can this be linked with well known equipment or products and is it possible to enlist the support of a manufacturer?

Time and money will be involved but if you have both to spare and are committed to the idea then above all things it must be done properly.

First of all it will be necessary to bring in the local press and if a manufacturer is involved probably more than that. The press will require advance information and the promise of a good feature item for the paper, which must include photographs to be really effective.

If the event can be associated with some local interest such as fund raising for a local cause this will help with publicity. A purely local charity would have this interest but there are also many national and international organizations to which proceeds from the event could be donated. Money could be raised simply by a collection or by raffling goods and/or services, or by charging a small fee for an entrance ticket which would give the spectator an opportunity perhaps to win a free hairdressing or beauty service. Before considering these or any other fund raising ideas it will be necessary to check the legal position to be sure you will not be breaking the law. It is possible that your local authority will have a charities advisory officer whose job it is, among other things, to give advice on such matters. If not there is always the Citizens Advice Bureau.

Finally, even if the occasion does not result in lots and lots of new clients it can be great fun doing it and there will be the added satisfaction of knowing the proceeds have gone to a good cause.

Personal recommendation

It is a regrettable fact that more and more businesses of all kinds appear to depend less and less upon the quality and reliability of their products and/or services and more and more on persuasive advertising and aggressive selling to achieve their financial aims.

There is little doubt that in an industry which offers a quite personal service to the public, the best, and incidentally the cheapest form of publicity is the quality of the services provided and the social skills involved in presenting and carrying them out.

Personal recommendation has always been and probably always will be the best advertising tool at the disposal of the hairdresser and the beauty therapist. Always make sure therefore that your own clients have much to recommend.

Window display

An eye-catching display in the salon window will cost no more than the materials used to set up the display. The overall effectiveness of this will to some extent depend upon the actual siting of the window and the number of potential clients who frequent the area. A clear view of the window from both directions and a clear forecourt which will enable people to stand and take in the detail of the display without being jostled by other passers-by is ideal. Heavily congested areas with a lot of people and traffic is not the advantage it might at first appear to be due to the distracting effect of all that is going on and the need to keep moving. Nevertheless the window should always be made to appear attractive if only as an indication of what lies within.

Displaying qualifications

Professional qualifications, together with diplomas and certificates from trade schools nicely framed and displayed in a prominent position such as the reception area or the window space itself will suggest a level of expertise which cannot fail to impress at least some of the potential and existing clients. For many people it is probably true to say that the social environment of the salon and the end result of the service are the two primary factors which will ensure continuing patronage but nevertheless clear evidence of formal training and qualification will add a touch of authenticity to work which is already demonstrably good.

Advertising in the salon

Advertising may begin away from the salon in the local press, by distribution of leaflets, by demonstration or by some other means but it should not be allowed to end there. Once clients have been attracted to the premises there are many ways in which to continue the process of selling services and products.

The first point of impact will be the shop front and the window dressing. The salon owner or manager must put the services on display, which means more than a price list and a few bottles of shampoo in the window. Window display can be used to present a generally attractive appearance with a broad indication of the range of services offered within – and from time to time can feature particular trends or services currently fashionable or in keeping with current events. Time, money and effort spent on window dressing is never wasted otherwise many of the big stores would not retain on their staff display specialists for this very purpose.

Window space is valuable and should be used to the best effect to increase demand for services and consequently productivity within the salon. Avoid making your window look like a chemist's shop with bottles and packets of this and that, and above all never allow it to look like the space you use to store empty boxes and unused equipment. It is amazing how many hairdressers not only fail to make effective use of their window space in terms of the general appearance of the salon but also appear to be unaware of the publicity value of this relatively cost-free advertising opportunity.

The general appearance of the premises, the shop-front and the window display should be such that it will invite the potential client to enter. Be careful you are not unwittingly discouraging good potential custom by either an outward appearance which is too upmarket and apparently expensive or on the other hand distinctly downmarket and cheap. Some potential clients will hesitate to enter if they think it could turn out to be embarrassingly expensive while others will shy away from anything which suggests a low standard of service or poor hygiene.

Once inside the salon the advertising – good or bad – continues. The overall atmosphere of the salon – the neatness, tidiness, sense of order, social skills, hygiene, freshness of the air, temperature and many other things – will confirm or deny first impressions as the client proceeds through the various stages of the service.

The receptionist, stylists and their assistants can be a good or a bad advertisement. It is clearly a question of practising what you preach. Staff should set an example with an appearance which is neat and attractive, well groomed hair in tip-top condition, hair colour which carries the hallmark of skill and artistry, skin which is obviously well cared for and make-up which is flattering but never excessive and lastly well-manicured hands. Perhaps a lot to ask in the middle of a busy working day but what well turned out members of staff are saying through their appearance is 'what we have done for ourselves we can also do for you'.

House style

The question of suitable clothing for staff to wear during working hours is bound to be a contentious one. In these days of go as you please many people feel entitled to wear what they like, when they like and where they like. Nevertheless there is something to be said for attempting to maintain a reasonable house style which will identify members of staff and present an acceptable image. Clearly, if you are going to adopt a particular style of clothing it will be necessary to

* state this as a condition when engaging staff;
* charge the cost of the clothing to business expenses.

In the first instance it is essential that staff should know exactly what is expected before accepting the post, and in the second

it would be quite unreasonable to expect staff to meet the cost
of items of clothing which they would wear only in the course
of their duties.

If this is a new policy which has to be introduced to existing
members of staff it will be advisable to proceed with great
caution and to seek their willing cooperation through prior
consultation. You will need to convince them of the good
sense of what you are proposing and may even have to compromise a little on the final style to be adopted. It is important
to get at least senior members of staff on your side and enlist
their support in getting general acceptance. Obviously there
will be an almost infinite choice of styles and colours but
provided attitudes are not unreasonable on either side it
should not be too difficult to come to a broadly acceptable
decision.

Virtually all of the large organizations which function very
much in full view of the public, such as hotels, supermarkets,
multiple stores and the like insist on a housestyle as part of the
overall business image and as this undoubtedly costs them
quite a lot of money they must believe it is worthwhile to do so.
If the large and successful business finds it necessary to give so
much attention to every detail of its image perhaps the smaller
business would be wise to do the same.

Display aids

Display aids to selling specific services can be provided
almost anywhere in the salon but they will be most effective
when placed strategically at a point of sale. Some people feel
that the best place for such material is in view of a dryer bank
or wherever clients are *waiting for processes to take* because
here they have a captive audience. In fact this is not generally
true because by now almost all major decisions will have been
made and the chosen process is under way or nearly completed. The only value at this point would be in respect of
future bookings or products which may be purchased through
reception when leaving. The most effective point of sale for
services is between reception and the position to which the
client is first taken because that is where most of the decisions
will be made. The final point of sale comes on return to
reception where the next booking is made and where hair and
skin products for personal use are on display.

Avoid overloading points of sale with material which is too
detailed or in too great a variety. The human mind can only

take in so much information at any one time and so it is better to concentrate on a simple but telling message which stimulates interest and invites further enquiry.

Finally, remember that there is a significant difference between the arriving client and the departing client. In the case of the departing client the die, or dye for that matter, has been cast and it is essential that the client should be pleased with herself and with the salon, for then she will assuredly come again. The arriving client is somewhat different for here all is anticipation and important decisions have yet to be correctly made and the service successfully carried to her satisfaction if she is to become yet another happy departing client.

Financial management

There are two kinds of accounting used in business:

* financial accounting;
* management accounting.

Financial accounting is another way of saying 'keeping the books' and is dealt with under that heading. Financial accounting is in simple terms a matter of recording accurately where the money comes from and where it goes to.

Management accounting is dependent upon the information provided by financial accounting but is concerned mainly with the actual management of money and resources; with the consolidation and development of the business within the constraints of the financial situation. We often hear a woman who runs her home well described as a good manager, which generally means that through her skills the family derives the maximum benefit from whatever financial resources there are. Management accounting is not, however, concerned only with existing resources but equally importantly with future resources for developing trade and increasing revenue. The home or business with a static income can probably do little more than pay its way and although this may be reasonably acceptable in the domestic situation it is hardly likely to be an adequate long-term position in the highly competitive world of business.

Financial control and liquidity

Businesses most commonly fail in their early years and the most common cause of failure is lack of financial control. The trader who waits until the end of the financial year to determine the true monetary position could find the business almost too far down the slippery road to insolvency to be saved. Even if it can be saved the amount of damage sustained may make it a long and difficult task to return to financial stability.

An understanding of the tools of financial analysis is the answer to controlling a business successfully. Anyone who has driven a car with a broken fuel gauge will know from experience that there is no way to be sure that the car will not run out of petrol perhaps miles from the nearest filling station. Similarly, to attempt to run a business without appropriate financial indicators will be equally hazardous. It is important to be able to summarize the overall financial position from time to time and this is normally done in business by preparing a financial statement or balance sheet. In simple terms the balance sheet summarizes what the business *owns* (assets) and what it *owes* (liabilities).

If the assets of a business exceed its liabilities it can be regarded as solvent but in real terms it is not quite as simple as this because whereas all liabilities, whether long-term or short-term, require to be met in cash within a given time scale not all assets are liquid (convertible into cash). Indeed a business can hold considerable assets and yet have problems of liquidity.

Liquidity

In simple terms liquidity refers to the availability of cash or assets which can be quickly and easily converted into cash. Cash is the most liquid of all assets but debtors and stock are also classified as liquid assets because hopefully debts will be paid and stock used or sold. It is self-evident that although a trader may have many debtors and a considerable volume of stock if there is little or no money in the bank a lack of short-term liquidity can cause very real difficulty. The expensive television and video in your lounge at home may be valuable assets but if you haven't the cash to pay the electricity bill – what then?

Assets

It is important to understand the nature of assets in relation to liabilities.

Cash or some means of quickly generating cash comprises the most valuable assets in immediate terms.

The value of fixed assets such as premises, furniture, fittings and equipment cannot normally be converted into cash but they do make an indispensable contribution to the generation of revenue.

Stock and debtors are two examples of current or liquid assets which can hopefully be converted into cash in the course of time but if the stock is not being used or sold and the debtors do not pay up they are of no immediate use and could eventually even become a loss.

The most useful asset is cash in hand or in the bank and is the most liquid of all assets because it is immediately available for use.

Cash flow

Cash management is vital in any business. A business must be in control of its cashflow if it is to survive. In simple terms cash flow means the money which flows into and out of the business. If cash outflow exceeds cash inflow over a period of time then the business will have what is known as a cash flow problem which if not corrected can lead to even more serious difficulties. There are two ways to correct this imbalance:

* to increase cash inflow;
* to decrease cash outflow.

It sounds simple enough but unfortunately there can be factors affecting cash inflow which are not entirely under the control of the management. These could include:

* a fall in the overall spending power of existing and potential clients such as a loss of commission, short time or even redundancy;
* other demands on clients' money which could include increases in rates, fuel and other household expenses, holidays, family needs, and even a new car;
* the strength of local competition;
* prices charged by competitors.

The majority of people have only a limited amount of money coming in and a great variety of goods and services compete for a share of that money. Not many people can have all they want and so choices have to be made. It is up to the hairdresser and the beauty therapist to provide services which will convince the majority of their clients of the confidence-building value of looking good at all times.

It would be naive to suggest that the answer to the problem of an imbalance between cash inflow and cash outflow is to attract more custom and/or increase charges because the former might not be possible and the latter might lose even more clients. If cash inflow cannot be improved then the immediate and hopefully temporary remedy is to look for ways of reducing cash outflow.

Cash outflow can be reduced in a number of ways, including:

* reducing overhead expenses where possible;
* avoiding overbuying of materials;
* reducing production costs;
* taking full advantage of suppliers' trade discounts and settlement terms.

Many overhead expenses cannot be reduced because they are fixed and contractual. However there are smaller miscellaneous expenses which it may be possible to trim and which may be running away with quite a lot of money. Perhaps one of the first things to do would be to make a careful examination of the petty cash book.

You may be using lighting where it is not really necessary and you could be wasting money by overheating the premises.

Is the stock figure too high? Too much money tied up in stock reduces cash available for other purposes. A common fault is overbuying of materials leaving large quantities of slow-moving stock which has to be paid for long before it is required for use.

You may have indulged in the purchase of equipment which is not truly effective, frequently unemployed and even redundant. You may have been tempted to buy too many items on extended credit and the instalments plus interest are eating away the profits.

Your production methods may not be truly efficient and more expensive than they need be. Staff may be wasting materials, hot water, electricity and other resources. You may be overstaffed for the volume of trading.

You may be missing out on suppliers' trade discounts, but beware overbuying just to obtain a discount, or you may be failing to settle accounts in time to qualify for a settlement discount. There may even be a discount for cash, and remember cash-and-carry is always cheaper than goods delivered.

Perhaps you have been riding on the good times and not given too much thought to the possibility of a reduction in trading level or an increase in costs and/or expenses.

Cash flow forecasting

In any business, large or small, it is important to be able to forecast future costs and expenses in relation to future revenue. In order to remain financially secure it is necessary to keep a watchful eye on revenue and expenses in order to maintain a sound cash position. Failure to look ahead can lead to a shortage of cash and supplies even when the business appears to be in a basically profitable period.

It will be helpful to set down as accurate a forecast as possible of what the trading and profit and loss accounts are expected to look like in six months time. Figures for comparative periods in the recent past will be useful as a guide but care must be taken to allow for possible increases in costs and expenses and a lessening of trade which may not be immediately foreseeable. The resulting figures should be based upon known and anticipated costs and expenses and the revenue which may be reasonably expected to be generated in the period prior to due dates for payment.

It should not be particularly difficult for the manager of a small business to make a realistic monthly cash flow forecast bearing in mind that even though some accounts are due in advance while others are paid in arrear they all require settlement on the due date out of existing cash resources. For example, rates which are demanded in advance for the following period makes no difference to the inescapable fact that they must be paid now out of past revenue. The important point is that it is only bills due in the future which can be paid out of future revenue. To attempt to pay today's or even tomorrow's bills out of todays income is to live from hand to mouth. Cash flow forecasting needs to look much further ahead than that.

Regularly recurring costs and expenses will be relatively easy to recognize but the time between due dates will vary considerably. For example, wages in a small business will normally be paid weekly whereas telephone, gas and electricity will fall due quarterly and rates half yearly. Suppliers' 30-day accounts will fall due monthly and will need to be paid long before all of the goods or materials purchased have been sold or used to generate revenue. Cash-and-carry will be paid for upon collection. Clearly in the case of short-term dues adequate working capital resources are an essential support for the cash flow situation.

The current ratio

A business's ability to meet its immediate liabilities can be shown by relating its current assets to its current liabilities. If the current liabilities are not properly covered then the business is exposed to financial risk. In extreme cases suppliers may put pressure on by stopping further supplies and creditors in general may resort to legal pressure to pay up.

The current ratio can be found in the following manner:

$$\frac{\text{current assets (cash + debtors + stock)}}{\text{current liabilities}}$$

It should be noted that the numerical examples which follow are intended only to demonstrate the method of calculation or to make a particular point.

Let us suppose that the current assets are £6000 and the current liabilities £3000, thus:

$$\frac{6000}{3000} = 2$$

We have a current ratio of 2:1 which means that the current assets could cover the current liabilities twice and so there is no immediate liquidity problem. A ratio of 2 is regarded as an ideal optimum. Anything appreciably less than 2 is regarded as inadequate and would suggest that the business may have too much money tied up in stock and/or debtors.

A more realistic calculation suitable for a hairdressing or beauty therapy business whose stock consists mainly of materials which are not directly converted into cash by selling but used in the various processes and who do not normally have many debtors would be:

$$\frac{\text{Cash (in hand or in the bank)}}{\text{Current liabilities}}$$

that is, say

$$\frac{3000}{1000} = 3$$

which means cash is immediately available to cover current liabilities three times, a ratio of 3:1. Clearly at this moment in time such a business could be said to have more than satisfactory liquidity. It does, however, raise another question. Assuming the money is either in the form of actual cash or held in a current account in the bank, is it necessary or wise to carry so much money where it is not earning any return? No business organization would normally allow much money surplus to immediate requirements to lie idle. The most convenient and profitable way for the small trader is to keep it in a high-interest cheque account where it is readily available and at the same time earns interest at current market rates.

Should the current ratio reveal that current liabilities exceed current assets to any substantial degree, such as a ratio of 1:2 or 1:3 then despite the fact that revenue may continue to be generated if the majority of creditors required payment in the very near future the business would be unable to meet their demands. This kind of situation is a precursor to the state of bankruptcy and has caused the failure of many an outwardly promising small business. Clearly the current ratio is a most important tool in financial management and should be frequently used to ensure continuing liquidity.

Accruals

This is an accounting term and means that all income and expense must be included in the accounting period whether for cash or credit. It is self-evident that when calculating the current ratio at a given time creditor accounts due or nearly due but not yet paid must be taken into account as current liabilities, bearing in mind that most are paid in arrear and that the benefit of those goods and/or services has, in theory at least, already contributed to the current assets. To give a naive example, to calculate a current ratio today ignoring the fact that gas and electricity bills fall due in seven days time provides neither a true nor a useful indication of the financial position. The projected salon revenue for the next seven days can be taken into consideration but that should be expected only to contribute a seven day share of the cost with the greater proportion already in hand. Every form of credit should be considered whether it is a normal 30-day account or quarterly such as electricity or gas. They all have to be paid in the end and ideally out of revenue generated during the period they cover.

Schedule D income tax

It would be useful at this point to offer a warning to one-time employees now trading on their own account, self-employed, with regard to the method by which they will now pay income tax. A tax return is normally made in April or May covering the trading period up to the 5th April. A tax assessment will probably be received in September or October and this will normally become due in two instalments for payment on 1 January and 1 July in the following year. It is important to bear in mind that this money has already been taken in the period covered by the return and that 27 per cent of the profit (standard tax rate at time of publication) correctly belongs to the Inland Revenue. Provided that the available year's profit has been regarded as the profit after tax with the tax portion set aside then all should be well, but if the entire profit before tax has been spent there could be difficulty in meeting tax payment when due. It is only the profit remaining after tax has been set aside that is for spending.

The final accounts

The final accounts consist of the trading account, the profit and loss account and the balance sheet.

The balance sheet is not part of the double-entry system of book-keeping but simply a financial statement which summarizes the asset and liability structure of the business at a given point in time. At some other point in time, perhaps even as little as a week later, the position may be quite different.

The balance sheet does not reflect all of the strengths and weaknesses of the business. It is purely a list of what the business owns and what it owes at that time. It cannot show the market position of the business now or in the future and it says nothing about the value of the skills of its manager or employees. It does, however, contain material which can be used to provide more detailed information regarding the financial position of the business.

The trading account summarizes the revenue derived from trading activities and the direct costs (cost of production) incurred in carrying out the services and the cost of supplying sales products which together generated the revenue. The difference represents the *gross profit*.

The profit and loss account includes the gross profit and summarizes all legitimate business expenses incurred in the organization and running of the business. The difference represents the *pre-tax net profit*.

Gross profit percentage. The gross profit percentage can be calculated from the trading account figures by dividing the revenue into the gross profit and multiplying by 100, that is:

$$\frac{\text{gross profit}}{\text{revenue}} \times 100 =$$

Again it should be noted that the numerical examples which follow are intended only to demonstrate the method of calculation or to make a particular point, therefore:

$$\frac{3000}{6000} \times 100 = 50\%$$

shows that 50 per cent of the revenue generated is gross profit.

Net profit percentage. The net profit percentage can similarly be found by dividing the revenue for the same period into the net profit from the profit and loss account, that is:

$$\frac{\text{net profit}}{\text{revenue}} \times 100 =$$

or

$$\frac{1500}{6000} \times 100 = 25\%$$

shows that 25 per cent of the revenue generated is net profit.

Cost component percentages. Individual components of the cost of production such as labour, materials or electricity can also be expressed as a percentage of revenue.

The percentage cost of labour can be found by dividing revenue into wages, not forgetting to include employer's National Insurance contribution, that is:

$$\frac{\text{wages}}{\text{revenue}} \times 100 =$$

but is more usefully expressed as a percentage of the cost of production, that is:

$$\frac{\text{operative wages}}{\text{cost of production}} \times 100 =$$

or

$$\frac{2400}{3000} \times 100 = 80\%$$

which shows that 80 per cent of the cost of production is wages. This is about the figure to be expected in a labour-intensive industry such as hairdressing or beauty therapy. This would probably represent about 40 per cent of the revenue which is generally regarded as acceptable in this particular field of business activity.

The figure for cost of production can be obtained from the trading account.

Overhead expense percentages. Various overhead expenses such as rent, rates, heating and lighting can also be expressed as a percentage of revenue in a similar way, that is:

$$\frac{\text{rent}}{\text{revenue}} \times 100 =$$

and so on.

Many of these calculations can prove to be a valuable diagnostic guide to causes of a fall off in profitability while productivity remains constant or increases. For example a reduction in gross profit while revenue remains constant could be due to increased wages, cost of materials or electricity which have not been passed on to the clients. Similarly a reduction in net profit while gross profit remains constant could be due to an unrecovered increase in any one or more of the overhead expenses.

Return on capital employed. It is useful to be able to determine the level of net profit in relation to capital employed.

First bear in mind that capital employed represents the total amount of fixed and current assets at the disposal of and for the full use and benefit of the business.

The percentage return can be found by dividing the capital employed into the net profit and multiplying by 100, that is:

$$\frac{\text{net profit}}{\text{capital employed}} \times 100 =$$

or, for example

net profit £10 000

capital employed £36 000

$$\frac{10\,000}{36\,000} \times 100 = 27\%$$

The pre-tax profit of £10 000 shows a return on capital employed of 27 per cent.

10
Business growth and development

It is reasonable to suppose that natural growth will occur in any business which supplies a necessary product or service of consistently good quality. Since, however, there can be many unforeseen factors which can affect future levels of trading it is never a good thing to be complacent even when everything seems to be going well.

Many small businesses depend largely upon local custom and their prosperity is often a reflection of the prosperity of the people who live and/or work in the area.

The financial status of local custom is beyond the control of those who own or manage local small businesses and this is a factor which can change often slowly for better but sometimes quite rapidly for worse, as many have experienced where high levels of unemployment have suddenly arisen. Clearly the nature of local industry and the sources from which local population derives its income is a matter to be taken into account when considering a site for a new business, the purchase of a going concern or extending your existing premises.

The kinds of business in the vicinity can also prove to be helpful in attracting people to that area. For instance, suppose a salon is situated in a small group of shops in a largely residential area, one of which is a high-class bespoke dress-making business. Well-off ladies may travel considerable distances to visit the dressmaker and so take the opportunity to get their hair done at the same time. A nearby florist's may specialize in weddings, and a salon could exploit this by making a feature of hairstyles for brides and bridesmaids.

The potential customer's interest in, or perceived need for any particular service can be stimulated by suitable advertising and promotional methods, but how successful that may be will depend to a great extent on the age and lifestyle of those who live in, work in, or otherwise frequent the locality.

In these days of almost universal private transport many people may be persuaded to travel considerable distances for services not readily available in their own area but if their patronage is to continue they will need to be convinced by the result that it is worth the journey.

It has been said that the successful entrepreneur supplies what the public wants today and anticipates what they will want tomorrow. The danger of this particular philosophy lies in the possibility of denying individuals the personal freedom of choice by putting the pressure on to persuade them that what the organization has decided they want is in fact what they really do want. Some hairdressers may be undermining their long-term interests by too readily casting aside some time-honoured services which have always earned good money and pushing exclusively modern trends even when they are not particularly suitable for some of the clientele. This could prove to be risky in a business sense by too severely narrowing the range of services provided. There is no doubt that what is highly fashionable now will not remain in fashion for very long because its potential will be quickly exhausted and the search for something different will already have begun. Fashion is essentially cyclical in nature and what has been before will inevitably return again, even though it may be in modified form.

It is perfectly possible to enjoy the best of both worlds by providing most of the modern trends while maintaining the more traditional services for those who genuinely prefer them. The essence of a successful hairdresser, or beauty therapist lies in versatility: the ability to carry out to a satisfactory standard literally any service dictated by current fashion or by the personal needs or wishes of the client.

Again diversity is the keynote and a salon which offers only a limited range of services, however profitable they may be at the moment, cannot be surprised if when the client requires something they do not or cannot provide she will go elsewhere on that occasion and may not return.

Hairdressing and beauty therapy are personal services which demand a particular kind of relationship between operatives and clients. It is essential that the clients should have absolute confidence in the skill and integrity of the staff. A dependable, caring, professional attitude and a job well done will do more than any contrived publicity can possibly do to ensure returning clients for many years to come.

Continuing growth depends mainly on genuinely providing

for the clients' needs and wishes in a congenial environment at a fair price. Growth implies long-term development. The child grows into the complete man or woman by a slow process of maturing through learning and experience. Even then the end product is often largely a matter of chance, although some manage to make a better job of it than others. So take the time which is necessary to build your business on a sound foundation, learning by your mistakes and ready to admit, at least to yourself, when you have obviously got it wrong. If you do need to think again, take heart and remember that your mistakes will probably teach you more than your successes ever will.

Needs and wants

At one time commerce was based upon needs. Identify a need, supply it and you were in business. In many ways this is still true today and one primary purpose of market research is to gauge the extent of need. Clearly a hairdressing salon in the middle of Dartmoor would hardly be likely to prove a success – there simply would be no need for it.

Identifying the need would therefore appear to be a prerequisite to the possible introduction of a new product or service. But we are now into an entirely new ball game, which is quite simply to *exploit people's wants*. An important part of the process is to attempt to convince potential customers that they actually *need what they want* and even to create wants they have never even thought of before. Take a critical look at modern advertising in general and television advertising in particular and you will realize that this is true. You may believe that you are not personally influenced by such advertising but a sufficient number of people must be otherwise companies would not spend millions of pounds on it.

To return to needs and wants, it will make an interesting exercise to list separately in two columns your real needs and your apparent wants. Be honest with yourself and include in the needs column only those things which are real needs and you will find that it is far shorter than the wants column. Clearly this points to the size of the potential market in wants as opposed to actual needs. You may need your fringe cut because it is interfering with your vision but do you really need it coloured bright orange. The problem is that today's want can become tomorrow's need. A brunette may want her hair bleached platinum blonde now but will later need the roots retouched to hide an ugly regrowth.

Fashion trends have a strong influence on perceived wants. Many people want to be in the fashion and will sometimes go to irrational lengths just to achieve this apparently desirable state. If curly hair is in fashion then people with naturally straight hair will need some form of permanent curling if they are to avoid the necessity for frequent, perhaps daily, temporary curling. If the fashion continues then further permanent treatment will be necessary to take account of hair growth. That which started out as a want for curly hair has now become a need for as long as the fashion lasts. Many women dislike having their hair permed but will put up with the inconvenience and not inconsiderable cost for as long as it is necessary. During such time permanent waving, or more correctly permanent curling, can prove to be a reliable and profitable service. When curls are out of fashion need for the service will decline and revenue from that area will be reduced. However, whatever fashion may decree there will always be a demand from older women for this kind of service as a need rather than a want because it helps to keep their hair neat and tidy and saves them time and trouble.

Wants can prove to be very profitable but needs are the sheet anchor of a business, building permanent custom and achieving a stable base to support relatively unstable but nevertheless profitable current trends.

Wants are fickle and can change rapidly with changing times. The demand for fashionable substitute or additional colouring for hair will continue just so long as that particular fashion remains popular but as most hair eventually loses its natural colour and goes white with increasing years there will always be a demand for permanent colouring to disguise the loss. The former is clearly a want and the latter nearer to a need.

Suppose, for example, that in a village there is a small barber's shop which has been there for many years. Much of the area has an ageing population and although the barber does not make a fortune he gets a comfortable living catering for haircutting and shaving. Every morning there is a small group of men waiting for the salon to open and modest trade continues throughout the day. Wants have nothing to do with his business, the barber is simply supplying a need which is likely to continue for as long as hair grows on the head and face unless, of course, they all decide to grow long hair and beards.

Target clients

Once you have some knowledge of the surrounding area and its population it will then be possible to consider their possible needs and wants. Obviously if your salon is in an area with a largely ageing population you are not likely to have a great demand for exotic hair colouring or sun-tan treatments unless you can attract a sufficient number of younger clients from further afield.

Facilities for small children will be an advantage for young mothers able to visit the salon during normal hours. If there are factories or office blocks in the area it might be a good thing to provide lunch-time hairdo's or remain open after they have finished work. It may even be worth considering flexible opening hours to suit the needs of the local population. Clearly the lesson is that if you can identify and cater for a need that your competitors have overlooked then you have the advantage.

Staff participation and staff benefits

Good staff attitudes are an essential ingredient if a business is to grow. Staff must be seen to benefit from growth. Any growth which implies more work with little or no extra staff benefit is hardly likely to meet with an enthusiastic reception. In the larger industries we are all familiar with the often understandable workforce opposition to proposed changes which they consider will worsen their conditions. Financial reward is probably the main benefit to consider and since businesses generally view growth ultimately in terms of increased revenue and profits it is not unreasonable to suppose the workforce will take a similar position with regard to their own perceived interests.

Although working hours and conditions are covered by appropriate legislation there are without doubt many instances where the law is contravened in one respect or another either through ignorance or deliberate default. However, quite apart from the minimum legal requirements it always bodes ill for harmonious staff relationships to neglect their reasonable personal needs. The installation of obviously expensive equipment to increase profitability while ignoring a grievous lack of facilities for staff to take well earned breaks in some degree of comfort is hardly likely to endear management to staff.

In the current economic climate there is always a danger that some employers and/or managers could be tempted to make demands of their employees which they might not do in other circumstances, particularly where the workforce does not have a union to provide a collective voice in defence of their interests. Such an attitude can prove to be counter-productive in the long term for if a business is to grow and develop on a sound footing the employer, management and workforce must go forward together.

Finance and consolidation

Ideally, growth is financed out of surplus revenue, ploughing back into the business a proportion of the profits. Large-scale development involving structural alterations and/or the installation of expensive equipment may need money over and above that which profits can supply and this will generally mean borrowing by one means or another. Before becoming committed to such a project it will be advisable to carry out an analysis to determine the long-term viability of the scheme and the chances of recovering the outlay within a reasonable time span. If it involves borrowing money then it will be necessary to be sure that repayments and interest could be met out of current revenue until the new development becomes self-supporting. Once again you need to ensure that what promised to be an asset does not turn out to be a liability.

Consolidation of an existing position is an essential strategy in business. In warfare when a taskforce moves forward and takes a new position its first aim thereafter is to consolidate that position against possible counter attack. Business, and particularly big business, is not unlike a form of warfare carried out, it is to be hoped, according to the rules and with respect for the legitimate rights of the adversary. If you have invested hard-earned capital to secure a share of a particular market you will be entitled to take reasonable steps to protect your investment and keep that share which may well come under attack from competitors, particularly if it is a new and profitable development where either by foresight or just good luck you managed to get in first. It would be naive in the extreme to ignore the fact that sooner or later others will want a slice of that particular cake. Remember that all business is vulnerable to competition unless, of course, it happens to be a monopoly. The question now is how to keep that share of the market? The answer is relatively simple and lies in the word competition, that is by making certain that you continue to give a first-class service that is as good as and preferably better than that offered by others in the field, maintain competitive prices and above all keep that image constantly before the public. Bear in mind, however, that it is one thing to claim to offer a first-class service and quite another to consistently provide it.

11 Insurance protection

Insurance is an overhead expense which generally carries no real benefits other than peace of mind. Over the years you will probably spend quite a lot of money on insurance and never need to make a claim and even if you do will get back no more than the value of what has been lost. You will insure against fire and yet, hopefully, may never suffer that misfortune, but if a fire does occur then you will be eternally thankful for insurance. Clearly it is not so much a matter of whether you can afford to insure but *whether you can afford not to insure*.

Insurance protection

Insurance means paying for protection against the consequences of misfortune. Insurance will not prevent the event but it will generally compensate should it occur. While there is no advantage to being over-insured it is important not to be under-insured because in the event of loss or damage it may not be nearly enough to cover the cost of repairs and/or replacements. It is possible to insure for current replacement value at the time of the loss (new for old) but premiums will naturally be higher and in times of high inflation insurance companies may apply certain restrictions to protect their interests.

When assessing the need for various types of insurance it is important to consider what the position might be in the event of each possible misfortune were it not covered by insurance. When taking out insurance it is essential to know exactly what protection you are buying. Be sure to read the small print and request an explanation of anything you do not fully understand. Because insurance can be a competitive business it may be well worthwhile to shop around for quotations but be sure to deal only with well established companies.

Duty of disclosure

Insurance contracts are based on the same principles as any other contract but unlike some transactions the insured party is required to make full and accurate disclosure of anything which might affect the risk insured. It is, therefore, essential not only to make all appropriate initial disclosures but also to keep the insurers informed of any subsequent change in circumstances which may subsequently affect that risk. Failure to do this either intentionally or through oversight could lead to refusal to meet a claim. For example if the fire policy cover does not specifically include storage of inflammable materials and you subsequently decide to carry a stock of such materials without disclosing the fact then it could be that you are not covered should this lead to a fire occurring.

Consequential loss

It is important to consider cover for consequential loss. If covered only for material loss such as tools, equipment, and stock then you can only claim for their value and not for consequential loss of profits. This is important should the premises be damaged by fire or other means when you would want to claim for loss of profits and even, in the long term, loss of goodwill. If the premises were unusable for any length of time then you would probably find that you had not only suffered loss of property but loss of livelihood also.

Cover

Make sure you know the precise extent of cover and pay particular attention to any *excluded risks*. Do not place complete confidence in what may be termed an *all risks policy* without first looking carefully at its actual terms and conditions. *All risks generally means compensation for all loss or damage actually specified and in the circumstances set out in the policy.*

Proximate cause

The actual cause of a particular loss can be a crucial factor in a claim. Claims are generally based on one direct and operative cause, the proximate cause, which may not necessarily be specified in the policy. For example, if theft by an actual employee is excepted and goods are stolen from the premises by a third party you may not be able to claim if an employee can be shown to have been an accomplice and this participation is considered to have been the proximate cause of the loss.

Again it is important to be sure that unforeseen circumstances do not arise which could constitute an excepted risk. If for example the cover is for cash in transit where an employee normally takes cash from the salon to the bank by a stated direct route but on one occasion decides to take the money home, stay for lunch and visit the bank on the return journey and during that time is robbed, deviation from the normal route or an accepted procedure might be held to be the proximate cause and an excepted risk.

Notice of loss

Most policies require notice of loss to be given within a specified time and in any event the best time is immediately. Written notification is best, provided time is allowed for possible postal delay but be sure to give notice within the required time and in the manner required by the insurers otherwise you could jeopardize your claim.

Proof of loss. Proof of loss is generally required and in the case of a claim for loss of profits an assessment by auditors would be necessary.

Settlement

Settlement is usually negotiated with the insurers and their assessors and although sometimes this is quite a straightforward matter, if the settlement is substantial it can be complicated and take some time to conclude. In the meantime you may have to struggle on as best you can, which is one more good reason for maintaining capital reserves. Insurers have certain salvage rights and will generally claim possession of lost goods when found or damaged goods after settlement. It is, after all, perfectly reasonable not to be able to receive payment for lost or damaged goods and at the same time retain title to those goods.

Insuring the business premises

Leasehold premises can be insured by the landlord or the tenant or both. If the tenant is not required to insure by the terms of the lease then the landlord must do so. If it is the tenant's responsibility then it is important to pay the renewal premium on time otherwise there may be a breach of the insurance covenant. The landlord's insurance will normally cover only the fabric of the building and any fixtures or fittings which are included. The tenant will need to obtain the very necessary cover for the contents against loss or damage and this will include tenant's fixtures, furniture, fittings, equipment, tools, stock and any other associated items kept on the premises.

Burglary insurance

It will be necessary to obtain cover for loss or damage caused by theft involving entry or exit by forceful or violent means. Cover for shoplifting is not normally available. The insurers will almost certainly want to be satisfied that the premises are reasonably well protected against burglary and it is wise to enquire in advance with regard to their actual requirements.

Money insurance

It is possible to insure against loss of money by an employee but this does not cover theft by an employee, although this can be done through a fidelity bond or policy. Loss of money by an employee usually involves money in transit between your premises and the bank or post office or where the employee carries money otherwise in the course of employment. It is also possible to insure against loss of National Insurance cards.

Liability insurance

Normal liability insurance of goods or property covers your liability to employees or to the general public as employer, owner or occupier of the premises and generally covers the actions of employees except where fraud or criminal acts are involved.

Public liability insurance which is so essential to a hairdressing or beauty therapy business should cover claims which may be made by a third party (the client) in respect of injury, disease, or damage to their property but generally excludes injury to your own employees. Such a policy does not absolve you or your employees from the Common Law duty of care. It is not, therefore, a licence to take chances on the doubtful assumption that the insurance company will pay up whatever happens.

Compulsory insurance

If an employee sustains injury in the normal course of employment the employer is generally held responsible whether or not personally at fault and is legally required to take out appropriate insurance with recognized insurers under the Employers' Liability (Compulsory Insurance) Act 1969. There are possible exceptions to this requirement such as when employing only members of the family. The certificate of insurance must be prominently displayed on the premises and provided employees can be shown to be properly trained and trustworthy the insurers cannot refuse a claim.

Personal accident and/or sickness insurance

It is possible to provide a scheme to cover accident or sickness as an additional benefit for employees and probably wise to consider health insurance for yourself if you make a substantial personal contribution to the productivity of the business.

Fidelity policies can cover against loss through dishonesty of employees and where specifically included against the consequence of their negligence.

Plate glass insurance

If the salon is situated at street level with a plate glass front it is important to make sure this is properly covered either by the landlord or through your own insurance. Glass is an expensive material and replacing a large expanse could prove to be very costly indeed.

Other kinds of cover

Provided you can afford the premiums it is possible to insure against almost any conceivable risk and to cover almost any foreseeable circumstance. Insurance companies and insurance brokers are always ready and willing to advise on insurance matters and any protection you may think you need but it is as well to bear in mind that their interests and your interests in the matter are not quite the same.

12 Costing

Accurate costing is one of the most important aspects of the financial organization of a business. Methods of costing will vary with the nature of the business but the main information required will be broadly the same. In a hairdressing or beauty therapy business it will be necessary to identify the:

* direct costs of producing the individual services, known in total as the *cost of production*;
* general expenses associated with the running of the business and known in total as the *overhead expenses*.

When a salon owner sets out to determine the price to charge for a particular service it will be necessary to know two things:

* the direct costs attached to actually producing that service;
* the proportion of general overhead expenses which must be allocated to that service.

Costs of production and overhead expenses will vary from salon to salon and from year to year. Therefore it should be noted that all figures given in this chapter are purely imaginary and intended only to demonstrate the principles of costing and the methods of calculation.

Because hairdressing and beauty therapy businesses are highly labour-intensive the greater part of the cost of production will be labour cost and most if not all of the revenue will come from the operative staff.

It is important to bear in mind that all costs and expenses involved in providing for and carrying out the services must be recovered from the clients before any question of profit can be considered.

Costs of production will include

* labour;
* materials;
* gas and/or electricity for heating water and operating equipment;
* laundry.

Overhead expenses will include:

* rent;
* rates;
* lighting;
* heating;
* telephone;
* cleaning;
* insurance;
* advertising;

and possibly:

* wages of a non-operative receptionist;
* salary of a non-productive manager.

Everything and everyone not directly productive must be regarded as an overhead expense and not a cost of production. It is very important to distinguish between these two categories.

Overhead expenses

First let us deal with the overhead expenses. There are several ways of doing this but the simplest way is to reduce the total overheads to an hourly rate, often referred to as the labour/hour rate, and although what follows is a modification of a rather more complicated procedure which would have to be used by a large manufacturing concern with many departments and many activities, it will serve our purpose perfectly well. The general principle is that the total for overhead expenses is expressed in relation to the total number of productive hours worked in a year and the appropriate oncost per unit is based on the labour/time element in individual output. If that explanation seems to be difficult to grasp do not worry because all will become clear as we proceed.

In hairdressing and beauty therapy those directly concerned with carrying out the services are the operatives and even though assistance may be provided by apprentices or trainees, the operatives are the actual producers of revenue. Therefore in calculating the proportion of overhead expenses the labour hours of fully operative staff only should be used. The calculation must be based on annual hours and annual overheads to take account of seasonal variations, that is the busy times, the not so busy times and the positively slack times. Also while rent and rates will not normally vary throughout a given year the cost of heating and lighting will certainly do so in accordance with seasonal conditions.

Now let us take an example by supposing a certain salon has 5 operative hairdressers and 2 apprentices working a 5 day 40 hour week. For present purposes we can ignore the apprentices because they are not the actual producers:

5 operatives × 40 hours = 200 hours

200 hours by 52 = 10 400 hours

Annual hours 10 400

The arithmetic is correct but we have overlooked two things:

* they do not work 52 weeks in the year – they take holidays
* there will not be customers receiving service from every operative during all of the hours – there will be 'waiting time'

Let us apply a correction for holidays and say that this will amount to 5 weeks in the year

52 − 5 = 47   200 hours × 47 = 9400

A correction must now be made for non-productive hours. Non-productive hours will vary from business to business and so we can only make an imaginary estimate. Let us say that over the whole year 20 per cent of the hours are non-productive, that is 2 hours in every 10 over the whole year. It could, of course, be more or less than this. Many owners would be reasonably satisfied with no more than 20 per cent non-productive time:

9400 − 1880 = 7520 productive hours

In order to find the actual figure to be added to service charges to recover overhead expenses we need to know the total annual expenses which will include rent, rates, lighting, heating, telephone, cleaning, insurance and so on. When this total is divided by the total productive hours it will show the hourly proportion to be added to charges. If, for example, the overheads amount to £10 000 per annum, then:

$$\frac{£10\,000}{7520} = 1.329$$

or when rounded up £1.33p per hour.

The foregoing example of costing to recover overhead expenses is based on the time taken for one operative to complete the process. It is clear that clients may overlap and that other processes may be started or finished during some of the time. For example, during the time taken to complete a permanent waving service the operative may carry out parts of another service while waiting for processing or while routine components such as neutralizing or shampooing are being carried out by an apprentice. It must be assumed, however, that there will be occasions when there is neither the need nor the opportunity to fit in other clients and the operative will be concerned with the one process for the whole of the time.

If a permanent waving service normally takes 2½ hours then the overhead expenses proportion must be applied over the whole time in order to be certain of recovering the full amount, that is:

the hourly rate multiplied by 2½

or

£1.33p × 2.5 = £3.32p

Cost of production

Let us now consider the cost of production. To find the labour cost, a method of calculation similar to that used for overhead expenses will be appropriate. The total cost of labour is reduced to a labour/hour rate and then used as the labour/time element in individual output. On this occasion the apprentices' or trainees' time is included because although at this stage they are not strictly productive their time has to be charged somewhere and as they are being trained as future operatives they are closely associated with production, therefore

5 operatives + 2 apprentices = 7 × 40 hours = 280 hours
280 hours × 52 = 14 560 hours.
Annual paid hours = 14 560

In this case there is no need to apply a correction for holidays or for waiting time because what is required here is the hourly cost of employing the productive staff regardless of whether they are working, waiting or on holiday. In calculating the unit charge for overhead expenses we required only productive hours whereas for labour cost we require paid hours. Bear in mind that there may be a substantial difference between productive hours and paid hours and that labour cost is based upon paid hours.

For example

paid hours	14 560
productive hours	7 520
non-productive hours	7 040

Thus the fully productive staff of 5 are required to produce sufficient revenue in 7520 hours to cover 14 560 paid hours plus other costs which we will look at shortly.

The total labour cost must now be reduced to a labour/hour rate and then charged as a labour/time element in the individual output.

As the total paid hours must be recovered out of productive hours it will now be necessary to divide the productive hours into the annual gross wages bill for the 5 operatives and 2 apprentices. Let us assume that the weekly gross wages bill for the 7 staff amounts to £500. Therefore:

£500 × 52 paid weeks = £26 000 annual gross wages

and so

$$\frac{£26\,000}{7520} = £3.46\text{p per hour}$$

If we now apply £3.46p per hour to the average of 2½ hours required to complete a permanent waving service, that is:

£3.46p × 2.5 = £8.65

It is interesting to observe that when this labour cost example is applied to a permanent wave costing the client £20 the labour cost percentage is in line with the accepted overall labour cost as 40 per cent plus of the revenue or turnover, that is:

$$\frac{£8.65\text{p}}{£20} \times 100 = 43\%$$

If the employer's contributions to National Insurance was not included in the wages bill it will be necessary to calculate the annual cost and divide by the number of productive hours to find the hourly rate.

In the above calculations we could have divided the wages of each individual member of staff by their productive hours but as they are probably paid at different rates for the same number of hours this would give a different charge to the service according to who was carrying it out. Clearly what is required is an average labour cost per hour for all services regardless of who is doing the work.

Commission

Some salons pay commission directly on individual takings after the operative's wages have been taken. As commission would be included in the annual wages bill this will be recovered in the labour/time element.

Cost of gas and/or electricity

It should be noted that the cost of gas and/or electricity for operating equipment and heating water is strictly a cost of production but because it would be inconvenient to separate this in the suppliers' accounts from the cost of lighting and space heating it is easier to allow it to be recovered in the overhead expenses calculation. Nevertheless it is perfectly possible to calculate the precise cost of operation for the purposes of general information by using methods which are described in the pages which follow.

Materials

The cost of materials must be calculated separately in accordance with the type and quantity used for each kind of service. Here we do not think of time but an average cost of materials for that service. It is often necessary to arrive at an average cost because the quantity used may vary from person to person and occasion to occasion. Any remainders which cannot be used are included in the charge.

It would be possible to increase the charge to an individual where an extra quantity was required but for the sake of happy relationships with clients in general, who may compare notes together, it is better to work to an average and treat everyone equally.

Although the majority of the materials used will be included in the stated price for the service there are sometimes items which are optional extras, such as special shampoos or conditioners. These items are generally charged directly to the client by adding the cost to the bill, but *be sure they are optional and that the client knows about it in advance*. In the long term it is always good business policy to state clearly basic prices and equally clearly indicate any extras which could arise. Very few people will be happy to find that they are eventually being asked to pay appreciably more than they had anticipated or been led to believe would be required.

When calculating the cost of materials do not overlook small incidental items such as cotton wool, tissues, ear caps, in fact any disposable items which have to be bought and must be recovered in the service price.

Laundry

Where a laundering service is provided on the premises the cost of hot water and electricity is already included in the overhead expenses proportion. If an independent laundry assistant is employed the wages will also appear under overheads. Therefore all that is now required is to recover the cost of materials such as washing powder and fabric softeners but if these are purchased out of petty cash they will appear in the miscellaneous and general expenses account and become part of overheads.

Operating equipment

Although the cost of gas and electricity for water heating and operating equipment is already recovered in the overhead expenses proportion it is useful to be able to calculate the operating cost of individual items of equipment.

Electricity

The cost of operating electrical equipment is quite easily found by the following method.

All electrical equipment should carry a small attached plate which shows the loading in watts or kilowatts. Note that 1000 watts equals 1 kilowatt and that the kilowatt is often expressed in shortened form as kw. With the aid of a small calculator – or in your head – it is not difficult to calculate the hourly cost of operation. For example a hand-held hairdryer may be marked with a rating of 1000 watts or 1 kw. This means that the dryer will consume 1 kw of electricity in every hour of continuous use.

The basis for calculating the unit cost of electricity is the *kilowatt hour*, which means that a 1 kw electrical appliance operated continuously for 1 hour will consume 1 unit of electricity, or:

$$1 \text{ kw} \times 1 \text{ hour} = 1 \text{ unit}$$

Let us suppose that the electricity undertaking charges 6p per unit for electricity supplied. This means it will cost 6p to operate a 1 kw electrical appliance continuously for 1 hour, or:

$$1 \text{ kw} \times 1 \text{ hour} \times 6p = 6p \text{ per continuous hour}$$

similarly:

$$2 \text{ kw} \times 1 \text{ hour} \times 6p = 12p \text{ per continuous hour}$$

This can easily be reduced to a unit/time cost, for example, if it takes 30 minutes to blow dry an average head of hair using a 1 kw hairdryer the cost of electricity will be 3p, or:

$$\frac{1 \text{ unit} \times 6p}{2} = 3p$$

The loading will vary on different items of equipment but once this is known it is a simple matter to calculate the hourly running cost. Some electrical appliances such as a washing machine, a tumble dryer or a water storage heater may carry loadings as high as 3 or 3.5 kw. The calculation is done in exactly the same way, that is:

$$3.5 \text{ kw} \times 1 \text{ hour} \times 6p = 21p \text{ per continuous hour}$$

Gas

With some gas appliances the manufacturers will supply information regarding performance and approximate operating cost but in general the only way to measure actual gas consumption is to operate the appliance on site and to take meter readings at the beginning and the end of the trial.

Reading the meter. The older type of gas meter registered the volume of gas consumed on a series of dials but the majority have now been replaced with a straight-line digital counter, that is:

$$2\;6\;8\;4\;8 \quad \text{or actually} \quad 2\;6\;8\;4\;.\;8$$

The first four figures are in black and the last in red to indicate this is the decimal figure. It is usual to read the first four figures and ignore the decimal which will carry on to the next reading.

If a reading is taken at the beginning and the end of a given period and the first reading is subtracted from the second we have the volume of gas consumed on that occasion, thus

$$
\begin{aligned}
2\,6\,9\,6 \quad & \text{second reading} \\
2\,6\,8\,4 \quad & \text{first reading} \\
\hline
1\,2 \quad & \text{gas consumed}
\end{aligned}
$$

Because the meter registers in 100's of cubic feet the figure of 12 really represents:

$$12 \times 100 = 1200 \text{ cubic feet}$$

The volume of gas consumed in a quarter would be much more than this, particularly when gas provides both hot water and central heating. In a winter quarter it could be as much as 50 000 cubic feet costing about £192.

Calculating the cost. The price of gas is based on a unit known as the 'therm'. The therm is equal to 100 000 British Thermal Units (or Btu's). To convert cubic feet into therms it is necessary to multiply the number of cubic feet by the calorific value of the gas, which is normally stated at the foot of the gas account, and divide by 100 000 which is the number of Btu's to a therm, for example:

$$\frac{1200 \times 1010}{100\,000} = 12.12 \text{ therms}$$

However, since the actual meter reading is expressed in the shortened form of 100s of cubic feet it is simpler to use the shortened equation which will produce the same result, that is:

$$\frac{12 \times 1010}{1000} = 12.12 \text{ therms}$$

It is now necessary to know the price charged per therm and this can also be found on the gas account. Let us say it is 38p per therm, and so:

$$12.12 \times 38p = £4.60p.$$

Profit

Only when the cost of production and proportion of overhead expenses has been determined can the profit margin be considered. The final level of profit represents the difference between the total cost of providing for and carrying out the service and the price charged to the client. So far we have been concerned to examine a standard approach to costing which is designed to show in fairly precise terms just how much a particular service will cost. This does not mean, however, that the price ultimately charged to the client can be equally precisely defined. Sometimes a too rigid approach to price formulation may lead to some services being needlessly underpriced while others may be overpriced. There are two ways of avoiding this situation, that is to:

  * adjust the price charged to the client by varying the percentage of profit from one service to another; or

* vary the proportion of overhead expenses to be charged to one service or another.

The cost of production attached to any individual service cannot be so adjusted.

It may be expedient on occasion to allow a popular and remunerative service to bear a greater proportion of overhead expenses in order to provide the means to subsidise some other service which has a higher cost of production or which it is considered desirable to promote.

Clearly, regardless of the method of adjustment chosen, the final objective is to establish a pricing policy which will ensure that the combined margins across the full range of services are, in total, sufficient to cover all direct costs of production and all overhead expenses and leave an acceptable overall margin of profit.

Market forces

Market forces operate in respect of all kinds of businesses which trade in a free market. It has been said of free enterprise that the level of profit can only be that which the current market conditions will allow.

Competition is one of the strongest market forces, where the prices which can be obtained for goods and/or services are influenced by competitive sources offering the same kind of thing. Competitive elements can involve price, quality, presentation and advertising.

The marketing pressures acting upon a hairdressing or beauty therapy business are most likely to include local competition, financial status of available custom and the clients' interest in or perceived need for any particular service.

While it must be admitted that what the client can afford or is willing to pay can have a profound effect on prices, any service which does not cover its cost of production, an appropriate proportion of the overhead expenses and provide an acceptable margin of profit must of necessity be kept under very careful observation. A sure recipe for disaster would be to follow the advice of a young lady answering a recent management examination question who wrote: 'charges should be what every customer can afford and in any case less than the salon down the road'.

13 Keeping the books

No owner or manager who wishes to control and direct the affairs of a business can possibly remain in ignorance of the financial aspects of its operations. While the skilled artisan may not have the time or inclination to master the complexities of advanced accounting – and for the size and type of business envisaged such expertise is hardly necessary – it is still essential to understand the purposes of primary accounting documents and know their value in ascertaining the current economic position of the business, and as a predictive tool for determining the viability of further progress and development. It is also desirable that the person responsible for the financial wellbeing of the enterprise should acquire an adequate level of numeracy and a working knowledge of book-keeping.

In terms of the average small business (sole trader) the keeping of accounts is often seen as a tiresome necessity for the purposes of satisfying the Inland Revenue and indeed this provides the main pressure on the owner of such a business to keep adequate books and records. The registered company falls into a different category and is required to keep full accounts for submission to interested parties. Since it is not possible to go into the complexities of company accounting the interested reader is advised to consult other sources of information and if contemplating the formation of a company to consult a solicitor and an accountant at the outset.

Why keep accounts?

There are several good reasons why even the smallest business should keep accounts, quite apart from the statutory requirement to submit appropriate aspects of financial affairs to the Inland Revenue whose duty it is to ensure that you contribute no less, and hopefully no more, than your proper share of the national tax burden. Perhaps the most important reason in terms of solvency is to be able to determine the current trading position of the business and gain early warning of any need for remedial action. Another important reason is concerned with controlling what is happening or likely to happen in terms of productivity and profitability.

Why keep so many different accounts?

In order to answer this question it is necessary to examine the purposes for which the various accounts are kept. To begin with a cash account or a cash book is used to record all money received into the business and all money paid out. It can show quickly at any time how much real money is available in the form of a balance. What it does not show is money which is owed to the business, or money which the business owes. Neither does it show precisely where money comes from, nor how it is earned or for what exact purpose money has been spent; it merely records receipts and payments. Therefore it is necessary to keep other accounts which will provide a record of what the business owes and what is owed to the business, what the business has bought and what the business has sold. Nominal and personal accounts will do just that.

For example a rent account will record matters of rent and will show at a glance what has been paid and what is due. Equally, suppliers' accounts will record all transactions with particular suppliers and show immediately what has been paid for and what is still outstanding. In general, ledger accounts keep separate records of the many different transactions with many different agencies for quick and easy reference when required. A record of the goods and materials in the salon stockroom will show how much actual stock there is but it will not as a rule show where the items were obtained, how much they cost or whether they have yet been paid for. Only a purchases day book and individual ledger accounts will do these things.

It is of great importance – if only for the sake of peace of mind – to know that the business is soundly based and clearly paying its way. Anyone who does not have an accurate knowledge of what their assets and liabilities are at any time, or has to wait for a bank statement to know exactly how much money they have, or finds a letter from the bank manager saying the account is overdrawn to be an unexpected shock, is likely to spend most of their business and/or private life going from crisis to crisis.

It is to be hoped that a sensible person would not attempt to cross a busy street without looking carefully both ways. To attempt to manage a business without adequate knowledge and understanding of its financial affairs would be rather like crossing a busy street wearing a blindfold.

As the ultimate purpose of a business is to make a profit and as every transaction plays its part in determining that profit, or loss, accurate accounting is essential.

An important point in the study of book-keeping is to distinguish and separate the business from the owner. Books must record all transactions from the point of view of the business. Whatever part the owner (trader) plays in the business organization it must be carried out on behalf of the business and not in a personal capacity. The owner may be completely convinced of owning the business lock, stock and barrel, but so long as the business has creditors then at least part of the assets belong to those creditors. Anyone who has suffered the misfortune of bankruptcy will have been left in no doubt of this fact, and in the case of a sole trader, and most partnerships, not only are the business assets at the mercy of those to whom money is owed but often the owner's personal assets also.

Double-entry versus single-entry book-keeping

Many small sole-trader businesses use a single-entry system of book-keeping and while this may be sufficient to meet the requirements of an Income Tax return has many disadvantages. It is inevitable that if and when the business expands it will be necessary to change to the double-entry system. In the case of a partnership or a limited company the latter method is essential from the outset.

The main disadvantages of single-entry book-keeping are that it is much easier for errors to be overlooked and it is by no means proof against fraud. It is also much more difficult to ascertain gross and net profits and the single-entry system cannot normally inform the trader of the ratio of the gross profit to revenue (turnover) or the relative proportions of the various overheads which represent the difference between gross profit and net profit. While single-entry book-keeping can provide some financial accounting of the simplest kind it is quite unsuitable for management accounting.

Double-entry book-keeping

It is not possible within the confines of this book to include a course of instruction in double-entry book-keeping. Readers who are studying salon management and business organization should find instruction in elementary double-entry book-keeping included in their course. Knowledge of book-keeping can be acquired with the aid of a suitable book but this is generally more difficult than by direct instruction. Many Colleges of Further Education offer part-time day and evening courses in book-keeping and the aspiring manager would do well to consider taking up such an option.

In the pages which follow it is the author's intention only to outline the general principles of double-entry book-keeping, to define types and purposes of various accounts and records used and to indicate how they relate to financial and management accounting.

Some basic rules of double-entry

All business transactions involve both *giving and receiving*. The term *giving* is not used in the sense of *a gift* but is an exchange of goods or services for money. This is a reciprocal arrangement where the trader gives and the customer receives the goods or services. In return the customer gives the money and the trader receives it.

If a small boy decides to purchase chocolate from John Candy, who keeps the local sweetshop, the transaction will be as follows:

* the boy receives the chocolate and gives the shopkeeper (trader) the money in return;
* from the other point of view, the shopkeeper gives the boy the chocolate and receives the money in return.

The boy could now open an account to record this transaction but first he must know an important rule of double-entry booking, which is:

* always credit an account when it gives;
* always debit an account when it receives.

This is John Candy's Personal Account seen from the boy's point of view:

John Candy's account

debtor (receives)	*(gives) creditor*
cash 50p	chocolate 50p

Note that two entries are made in the account, one on the right-hand or giving side because the shopkeeper gave the chocolate and one on the left-hand or receiving side because the shopkeeper received the money.

If John Candy decided to keep a boy's personal account he would see it from his point of view and it would look something like this:

Boy's account

debtor (receives)	*(gives) creditor*
chocolate 50p	cash 50p

The boy could also open a cash account to show income (pocket money) and expenditure (where the pocket money went). In this account he will record all money received and all money spent. Remembering our first rule, the cash account is debited when it is the receiving account – in this instance it is debited with the pocket money which it receives and credited with the payment to John Candy which it gives:

Cash account

debtor (receives)	*(gives) creditor*
pocket money 50p	John Candy 50p

Now let us suppose that the boy did not have the money to pay for the chocolate until he received his pocket money at the end of the week and that the trader John Candy was willing to supply the chocolate and wait for the money. John Candy's account will now look as follows:

John Candy's account

debtor (receives)	*(gives) creditor*
	chocolate 50p

John Candy is now the boy's *creditor* and the boy is John Candy's *debtor*. The creditor is the person or business to whom money is owed and the debtor is the person or business owing the money. At the end of the week, when the boy pays for the chocolate, John Candy's account will be debited with receiving the money.

Now let us suppose that it became necessary to close (audit) these accounts after the boy had received the pocket money but before John Candy had been paid for the chocolate. Remember that many business accounts will be in this position at the end of the financial year. In these circumstances the accounts will be balanced as follows:

John Candy's account

debtor (receives)		*(gives) creditor*	
balance c/d	50p	chocolate	50p
	50p		50p
		balance b/d	50p

Cash account

debtor (receives)		*(gives) creditor*	
pocket money	50p	balance c/d	50p
	50p		50p
balance b/d	50p		

Note that John Candy's account shows that he is still owed 50p by bringing the balance down on the credit side. Most purchases accounts involving credit transactions will show a credit balance at the end of the financial year. Real business accounts will naturally contain many more entries throughout the year.

Note also that the cash account shows a debit balance suggesting that the boy owns 50p – that he has an asset of 50p. However, he also has a liability of 50p because he owes that amount to John Candy.

Remember that an asset is something that a person or business *owns* and a liability is something that a person or business *owes*.

Regardless of whether the boy paid for the chocolate immediately (cash transaction) or at the end of the week (credit transaction), sooner or later a debit entry must be made in John Candy's account to show that he received payment. When this is done a corresponding credit entry can appear in the cash account. This points to the second important rule in double-entry book-keeping which is:

* for every debit entry there must eventually be a corresponding credit entry;
* for every credit entry there must eventually be a corresponding debit entry.

Every transaction requires a record of both giving and receiving which is the underlying principle of double-entry book-keeping. To put it another way

* all value (whether it is money, goods or services) coming into an account is debited to that account;
* all value (whether it is money, goods or services) going out of an account is credited to that account.

One of the primary purposes of keeping accounts is to show where value comes from and where value goes to. In the case of the boy we know that he received pocket money and we know how he spent it but this was a very simple transaction used merely to demonstrate basic principles. The financial transactions of a normal business would be much more complicated and would require many more records.

Normally in a business the money coming in (revenue) is derived from trading in one way or another. One of the most common forms of trading is by supplying goods and/or services. This will inevitably involve many transactions and a variety of accounts will need to be kept.

John Candy, as a trader, would need at least a sales account to record takings and if he sells on credit terms it will be necessary to have individual customer (debtor) accounts to keep track of money owed to the business. Suppliers' (creditor) accounts would be required to record goods bought and keep a check on money owed by the business. It would also be necessary to keep general accounts to record expenses incurred in running the business such as rent, rates, electricity and so on. At the end of the financial year, at least, John Candy would need final accounts including a trading account and a profit and loss account showing his gross and net profit.

In any small (sole trader) business it is not too difficult to keep accounts provided adequate time is allowed for the necessary paper work and all entries are carefully, accurately and, equally important, regularly made. While it is unlikely that the average small business could afford the services of a full-time book-keeper it is possible to engage the services of an accountant to prepare the trial balance, trading account, profit and loss account and balance sheet, and to advise on tax matters. Obviously this will prove to be more expensive than doing it yourself but if your knowledge of accounting is very limited it could turn out to be a saving in the long run. If you do engage an accountant it will save his time and your money if you have properly prepared all of the information he will need to draw up the final accounts. The more time he has to spend searching among your miscellaneous scraps of records for necessary information the more it will cost you.

Stock records

Stock records will need to be kept and the easiest way to do this is to enter the necessary details from the purchases day book covering each category of stock into a suitably ruled stock book.

Materials for use in carrying out salon services should be stored and recorded separately from products intended for direct sale to the public. This rule should be observed even though some of the items may be the same or similar.

Quite apart from keeping control over the stock itself figures for opening and closing stock will be required when the final accounts are prepared at the end of the financial year.

A stock room or at least a substantial cupboard is necessary for the storage of the main stock. It is essential that this should be kept secure and with controlled access. This is not to say that staff are or will be dishonest but it is better to remove the temptation for anyone to help themselves to a tube of this or a bottle of that, which many otherwise honest people consider today to be a legitimate perk.

Dispensary

It will be extremely useful if a separate dispensary or dispensing area can be provided as this may be used both to prepare materials and keep identifiable standard amounts of stock for daily use. The shelves can be topped up from the main stock as the items are used. Because of the relatively small standard quantities involved in this arrangement it will be possible to make a quick daily or weekly check. If, for example, the standard dispensary stock of a particular item is 10 and the staff is required to record each withdrawal then it is a simple matter to subtract the total number recorded from the standard number when the difference should tally with the remainder on the shelf. It should not be too difficult to devise a simple card system allowing a date for each day and requiring only staff initials against each item withdrawn.

It will be necessary to keep an accurate stock room record of standard issues to the dispensary. The need for reordering will be indicated when the current issue of any item to the dispensary leaves a predetermined quantity in the stock room sufficient to cover the foreseeable needs of the salon until a new delivery is made, but with reasonable allowance for possible delay in delivery.

The ledger and subsidiary books

The ledger is the backbone of the double-entry book-keeping system. The ledger could in fact contain all of the financial records necessary for running a small sole-trader business. In practice, however, as the range and volume of business grows it will be found to be more convenient to remove some accounts from the ledger and to use separate books. A prime example would be the Cash Book. It is also common practice to keep other separate books such as the wages book and the petty cash book which is used to record details of sundry small expenses which do not warrant separate ledger accounts. Summary totals would then be posted periodically to the Wages Account in the ledger and totals from the petty cash book to a miscellaneous and general expenses account. Note that the wages book and the petty cash book require their own summarized accounts in the ledger in order to conform to the double-entry system and allow accurate annual balances to be transferred to the appropriate final accounts.

Two other books known as books of first entry will also provide a means of recording details from which summary totals can be posted to appropriate ledger accounts. These are the purchases day book and the sales day book. In the case of a hairdressing or beauty therapy business which may provide both services and products for sale it will be more convenient to devise a services/sales day book with the receipts from either source recorded in separate columns.

For the average sole-trader hairdressing or beauty therapy business envisaged here it will generally be sufficient to use the following books:

* ledger;
* cash book;
* petty cash book;
* wages book;
* purchases day book;
* services/sales day book.

Ledger accounts

Many accounts can be opened in the ledger to provide records and information that a trader may require. It is possible to operate a very small business with a limited number of ledger accounts but as the business grows these accounts could prove to be both inconvenient and inadequate. For example, a single expenses account could be used and would contain a record of all of the expenses of the business.

A single expenses account might include rent, rates, wages, advertising, and other items. From such an account it would be difficult to separate totals for different types of outgoings. For example, rent is a business expense the annual balance (total) of which would need to be transferred to the profit and loss account, whereas operatives wages in a hairdressing or beauty therapy business would be a cost of production transferred to the trading account. Remember it is most important to distinguish between business expenses and costs of production. Costs of production are those items of expenditure which contribute directly to the product or service supplied, whereas business expenses (overheads) are items of expenditure necessary for the running of the business but not directly involved in actual production. Therefore, instead of all items of expenditure being posted to the one expenses account it is normal for items belonging to a particular category to be posted to their own separate ledger accounts, such as the rent account, rates account, wages account, advertising account and so on. Accounts of this kind are known as nominal accounts.

Trading accounts

The main trading accounts of a business are the purchases accounts and the sales accounts – accounts which record goods and materials purchased and goods and services sold.

The purchases accounts will show what the business owes to its suppliers and are generally known as creditor accounts. The sales accounts will show what is owed to the business by its customers and are generally known as debtor accounts. Accounts of this kind are also known as personal accounts.

In accordance with normal double-entry practice the trading accounts are credited when they give and debited when they receive. If, for example, goods are ordered from the Supercurl Company, when the invoice is received from that company details will first be entered in the purchases day book and totals later transferred to their account in the ledger on the credit or giving side. Eventually when the company is paid for the goods their account must be debited with receiving payment.

It will be necessary to keep individual accounts for all suppliers and to keep a purchases account in which summarized totals may be entered for easy transfer to the trading account at the end of the financial year.

The majority of businesses derive almost if not all of their revenue from selling either goods or services and sometimes both. Although it is easy to think of goods as being sold it is not always so easy to think of services in the same way but whatever we may do for a living we are trading in one way or another. The doctor sells diagnostic skill and the chemist sells the medications prescribed.

A business must keep records of goods and/or services sold and payments received in return. How are these sales to be recorded? The primary deciding factor is whether they are for cash or credit. Some businesses sell almost entirely on short-term credit, that is to say they are prepared to wait 30 days for payment and almost all hairdressing and beauty therapy suppliers operate on this basis.

Where goods and/or services are supplied on credit it is necessary to keep a personal account in the ledger for each individual customer (client) in order to keep track of money which is owed to the business, together with a sales account in which summarized totals may be entered for easy transfer to the trading account at the end of the financial year. As with purchases it will be more convenient to maintain a sales day book as a book of first entry into which sales may be entered daily for later posting in summarized form to the appropriate individual accounts.

The majority of hairdressing and beauty therapy sales involving goods and/or services are for cash and generally all that will be required is a sales day book and a sales account in the ledger. The sales day book should contain a sufficient number of analysis columns to allow receipts from different services to be entered separately with one additional column for products sold directly. All entries should be made daily. The separate columns are necessary to provide the means to determine the level of contribution to total revenue provided by each service and also from retail sales.

The cash book

Real cash is no longer the predominant means of paying for goods and services and when we speak of a cash transaction it often refers more to immediate payment than the use of coins and notes. When a customer pays by credit card it is to all intents and purposes a cash transaction. It is not the trader who gives the card holder credit but the organization which issues the card. Payment by cheque does not involve the giving of credit and this can generally be regarded as the equivalent of cash. Only account customers receive credit from the trader.

Today the bank account is commonplace and more and more people pay for their goods and services by cheque or by credit card. Of necessity an increasing number of quite small businesses now accept payment by credit card and it may be only a matter of time before all but the smallest transactions

will be completed by this or some similar method. Nevertheless we will probably continue to use the term cash book for
the means by which receipts and payments are recorded
regardless of the method used to transfer value whether it be
cash, cheque or credit card.

Receipts and payments can be recorded in a cash account in
the ledger or in a separate cash book. It is sometimes convenient to use a cash book which contains separate columns to
record cash in hand and cash in the bank. Some traders retain a
proportion of actual cash received as cash in hand to meet
small business expenses but it is more efficient to pay all
receipts into the bank and maintain a petty cash system for this
purpose.

It is essential to keep the cash book entries up-to-date so that
the balance at any time will truly reflect the amount of money
available for use.

Direct debit

Many people, privately and in business, find it convenient to
authorize their bank to make direct payments at given intervals
over a given period of time in respect of certain commitments
such as rates, gas, electricity and so on. This has the advantage
of spreading payment evenly over a longer period, avoiding
accounts being overlooked and, not least, avoiding the possibility of large bills appearing unexpectedly at inconvenient
times. Some people object to this system on the grounds that
they are making payments before they need and that the
money will be better in their own bank. However, this argu-
ment falls down unless you can be sure the money will be there
when needed and in the meantime kept where it will earn
worthwhile interest.

Where direct debit or similar regular payments are made it is
important to keep a record showing the dates on which individual payments will be made and to be sure to enter them
immediately in the cash book as they fall due.

Bank statement

At first sight a bank statement would appear to have turned
your double-entry system on its head by appearing to credit
money received and to debit money paid out. The simple
explanation for this apparent contradiction is that the statement is in fact a copy of the trader's account in the books of the
bank *seen from their point of view*. When money is paid into
the bank it is recorded in the trader's account as money

given to the bank to hold and because the account gives it is credited. When money is paid out by the bank to the trader's creditors through cheques, direct debit or other means it is regarded as money received by the trader and the account is debited accordingly.

As each bank statement is received it should be checked carefully against the cash book entries and the cheque stubs to be sure no errors have occurred on either side. The balances between the bank statement and the cash book will rarely be found to exactly agree because there are bound to be items which were entered in the cash book after the date of the bank statement and possibly cheques issued which have not yet filtered through to the bank. It will, therefore, be necessary to prepare a reconciliation statement which simply requires:

* the balance of the bank statement;
* plus payments-in which are not included;
* minus cheques drawn which are not included.

That is:

	Bank statement	Cash book
Balances	£160	£200
add payments-in which are not included	40	
	£200	£200
or		
Balances	£200	£160
deduct cheques drawn which are not included	40	
	£160	£160

In many cases there will be a combination of both plus and minus but provided the process of adding and deducting is correctly applied to the bank statement balance it should come out the same as the cash book balance which is, or should be, the most up-to-date record.

Non-trading accounts

Ledger accounts are required to record purchases of items which are known as fixed assets. Fixed asset accounts are different from trading accounts in that they merely record the acquisition of things which are kept for permanent use such as furniture, fittings, equipment and similar items which support trading activities but are not consumed as part of a process or resold in the normal course of business. Separate accounts can be opened in the ledger for each category of fixed asset, for example, a salon furniture account, a salon equipment account, a laundry equipment account and so on. Debit entries would be made in each case because the accounts would be receiving the assets. No entry is required on the credit side until the end of the financial year when each account will be balanced and the value of the assets transferred to the balance sheet.

Provision for depreciation account

An up-to-date method of dealing with depreciation of fixed assets is to leave the assets in their accounts at their original cost and open a provision for depreciation account which is credited annually with the amounts of depreciation. This account has the advantage that it shows clearly how much money must be set aside each year from profits to finance eventual replacement.

There are a number of methods by which depreciation can be calculated but one which is suitable for the sole trader and at the same time easy to apply is the straight line method, which is as follows:

* original cost of item;
* less estimated disposal value at end of useful life;
* divided by estimated number of years of useful life.

Or, for example:

	£
original cost of item	210
estimated disposal value at end of useful life	10
divided by estimated number of years of useful life	$\dfrac{200}{10} = 20$
depreciation at £20 per annum	

The question of depreciation and claims for capital allowances in respect of fixed assets is a complicated one and the trader is advised to seek relevant professional advice as necessary.

Fixed assets on credit

Where fixed assets are purchased on credit terms, only the actual cash price of the asset is entered in the relevant asset account. The interest charged for credit can be entered in an interest on credit account and eventually set against profits in the profit and loss account where it is allowed as a business expense.

The petty cash book

Petty cash is needed to cover various minor expenses which are:

* not sufficiently important to justify separate ledger accounts;
* too small to be conveniently paid by cheque.

The petty cash book will need to contain a number of separate columns to allow for recording these items under different headings. Initially a cash float is provided and is entered on the left hand or debit side of the book. Payments out are shown on the right hand or credit side and the compound totals of the various columns will be posted at given intervals to the miscellaneous and general expenses account in the ledger and eventually transferred to the profit and loss account as a business expense.

The Imprest system. The common procedure is to provide petty cash with a sum of money estimated to cover normal expenditure for a month. At the end of the month the credit balance is brought down to the debit side and further cash equal to the amount spent is entered to restore the balance to the original float.

Capital account

The capital account is the owner's account showing financial relationship with the business. This account records the owner's capital on the right hand or credit side and subsequently profits, or retained earnings, transferred from the profit and loss account. When the owner withdraws money from the business it is entered on the left hand or debit side and reduces the owner's financial holding accordingly.

Drawings account

The sole trader or owner does not receive wages or a salary but will need money for personal and domestic purposes and this is provided by making regular drawings against existing or anticipated profits.

Clearly if the owner is drawing against profits before they have been made then the money is reducing existing capital and care should be taken to ensure that such money is replaced from profits in due time. Here is yet another timely warning to the sole trader. Profits actual or anticipated are not yours simply to indulge in a grand holiday or a smart new car. By all means allow yourself a reasonable income (drawings) but also retain a proportion of the profits in the business for future development and to finance contingency reserves against leaner times or unforeseen expenses. *Above all, never, never live out of the till.*

The amount of your income depends on how much you think you are worth and necessarily how much the business can afford to let you take. Regardless of how you would like to dispose of the profits it is always well to remember that in law you, as a sole trader, and the financial affairs of the business, are inseparable. The debts of the business are your debts and you cannot normally escape that responsibility even to the extent of your own private possessions.

Always faithfully record all drawings by crediting the cash book, the giving account, and debiting the drawings account, the receiving account. In due course drawings are transferred to the debit of the capital account and the drawings account is credited with the transfer. The drawings account is important because it provides a convenient, or perhaps from some points of view inconvenient, record of the extent of the owner's drawings.

If items are supplied from stock for the private use of the owner this will effectively reduce the stock of goods or materials available for sale or use in the business by the cost price of the items withdrawn and this should be properly recorded and debited to the owner. All transactions, no matter how trivial they may seem to be at the time, must be properly recorded, and that applies just as much to the person at the top as it does to the youngest and newest member of staff.

Wages book

A wages book is required to record all matters connected with the payment of employees for the labour they supply. This will include the basic wage, overtime, commission and/or bonuses, together with compulsory deductions of national insurance and income tax, and any other voluntary deductions which have been properly agreed.

Employees must be provided with a statement showing the composition of the gross wage, all deductions and the final net wage.

Taxation

The sole trader will be involved in taxation as follows:

* PAYE Income Tax in respect of employees;
* National Insurance Contributions in respect of employees, together with employer's contributions;
* Personal National Insurance Contributions as a self-employed person;
* Value Added Tax in respect of trading purchases and charges for services and sales;
* Schedule D Income Tax in respect of the business profits.

PAYE Income Tax

PAYE must be operated for all employees whose rate of pay exceeds a specified amount which is known as the PAYE threshold. PAYE normally applies to *all gross earnings* regardless of the method and period of payment. Thus it applies not only to wages or salaries but also to additional payments such as commission and/or bonuses.

It is the employer's duty to deduct the required amount of tax from the pay of all employees who are not exempt. Failure to do this may entail a liability to pay over to the Inland Revenue any tax that should have been deducted, even though it was not, and may also incur certain penalties. Thus it is the employer's ultimate legal responsibility to pay the tax to the Inland Revenue and a matter of personal financial interest to ensure that it is correctly deducted at source.

Because of the complexity of the PAYE system and the ever-present possibility of changes in procedure the reader is advised to study the current issue of *The Employer's Guide to PAYE* (Leaflet P7 or its equivalent) together with Tax Tables and forms for operating PAYE published by the Board of Inland Revenue and obtainable free of charge from the local Tax Office.

National Insurance Class 1 Contributions

As with PAYE Income Tax it is the employer's responsibility to pay over to the Inland Revenue both the employer's and the employee's National Insurance Contributions. The employer is entitled to deduct the amount of the employee's contribution from pay. The employee's share is normally determined by the amount of gross earnings (earnings related) and the employer's share is at a fixed or standard rate. Contributions are payable only if the employee earns a certain amount or more.

PAYE Income Tax and National Insurance deductions must be paid over to the Inland Revenue within 14 days of the end of each tax month together with the appropriate return forms supplied by the Tax Office, which must be properly completed. Because of the complexity of the National Insurance system and the possibility of changes in rates and procedures the reader is advised to study the current issue of *The Employer's Guide to National Insurance* (Leaflet NP15 or its equivalent) published by the Department of Health and Social Security and obtainable free of charge from the local DHSS Office or the local Tax Office.

The sole trader's (self-employed) National Insurance contributions

All self-employed persons are normally required to pay Class 2 flat rate contributions, together with Class 4 contributions which are earnings related, which means how much is paid under this latter classification depends on the amount of the net profits from trading. Note that the net profits from trading are the trader's gross earnings, that is, before any personal deductions or allowances have been claimed.

Payment of Class 3 contributions is voluntary but it is worth looking into the matter because they could qualify for some benefits not covered by Class 2 and Class 4.

Class 2 contributions are either paid regularly by direct debit or by stamping a contribution card. Direct debit is obviously the most trouble-free method and avoids forgetting to stamp the card or even losing it altogether.

The actual amount of the Class 4 contribution is calculated as a percentage of the net profits which fall between a specified upper and lower limit. Class 4 contributions are normally assessed and collected along with Schedule D Income Tax.

If profits fall below a certain limit it may not be necessary to pay either Class 2 or Class 4 contributions but do not get too excited about that because the limit is somewhat on the low side of not very much.

Once again the reader is advised to study the relevant leaflets which are the *National Insurance Guide for the Self-employed* (Leaflet NI41) and *Class 4 NI Contributions* (Leaflet NP18) or their equivalents obtainable free of charge from the local DHSS Office or the local Tax Office.

All of the leaflets mentioned above are available under the given references at the time of publication but should the reference numbers and/or titles be changed appropriate current replacement documents will be supplied.

Value Added Tax

This is a tax applied to most business transactions which take place in the United Kingdom. Anyone in business with a taxable turnover (revenue), that is a gross turnover which exceeds certain limits becomes a taxable person and must register for VAT. Taxable turnover is the gross value of all taxable outgoing goods and/or services which represent the trading activities of the business. It is the person, not the business, which is registered for VAT and each registration covers the business activities of that registered person. The person registered can be a sole trader, a partnership (jointly or severally) or a limited company which is regarded for legal purposes as a person.

If previously untaxable turnover is considered likely to rise above the prescribed limit in the reasonably near future it is important to apply for registration in good time in order to avoid having to account for VAT before the actual date of registration. VAT is applicable from the date at which the taxable figure is reached and Customs and Excise can claim payment of tax from that date.

In a hairdressing or a beauty therapy business any applicable tax will be collected from clients by including it in the prices charged. This is known as *output tax*. In many businesses tax charged is required to be shown by issuing a tax invoice. Fortunately the majority of hairdressers and beauty therapists sell their services direct to the public for cash or its equivalent and do not need to issue a tax invoice unless specifically asked for one. It is essential however to record daily gross takings in a way that separates the tax element from the remainder of the charge. Thus at the end of the day it is a relatively simple matter to extract the output tax total.

The majority of businesses are charged VAT by their suppliers and for most purposes hairdressers and beauty therapists are no exception. The tax charged on incoming goods and/or services is known as *input tax*. The simplest way to record input tax is to provide a separate column in the purchases day book in which input tax charged on each incoming account (tax invoice) is separately entered. Thus at the end of a given period it is a relatively simple matter to extract the input tax total.

Bear in mind that it is most important to know if suppliers are registered for VAT (most will be) and to ensure that a proper tax invoice is received on each occasion showing the suppliers VAT number, the tax point date and the amount of tax charged. The tax point date is necessary because even if the account has not yet been settled the tax point date indicates the tax period in which the input tax is applicable.

Purchases from a cash-and-carry wholesaler will also need tax invoices or an equivalent document. If the wholesaler uses till slips instead of invoices and on which the goods are represented only by product code numbers it will be necessary to have a copy of the wholesalers product code list available for inspection when required.

The registered trader recovers from the customers the tax charged by the suppliers (input tax) in the tax charged to the customers (output tax). Any tax portion collected over and above the input tax is payable to the Customs and Excise.

VAT return. The VAT return is made on a standard form issued by Customs and Excise and the key entries on the form will be input VAT and output VAT. Customs and Excise do not require records to be kept in any particular way but they must be complete and up to date and the figures used to fill in the VAT form must be readily available when a VAT officer calls to examine records and accounts.

The VAT return mainly summarizes the totals of input and output VAT and arrives at a balance which will be either in favour of Customs and Excise or the trader. The difference is mainly in favour of Customs and Excise and this must be remitted no later than one month after the end of the tax period. Bear in mind that a trader is not entitled to deduct any item of input tax without a corresponding tax invoice.

Customs and Excise Account. It is important to keep a Customs and Excise account in the ledger to which monthly VAT inputs and outputs can be posted. Such an account will summarize the position and quickly show any balance which is due. It will also facilitate completion of the VAT return and help to satisfy the VAT officer that adequate records are being maintained.

The reader requiring VAT information in greater detail is referred to the list of official publications which can be found on pages 151–2 of this book.

Schedule D Income Tax

Income Tax paid by a business is calculated on its net profits which is the amount of trading revenue that remains after all legitimate costs and expenses have been deducted. It is the balance of the profit and loss account. The manner of calculation together with how and when the tax is required to be paid will depend on whether the individual is personally assessed as a self-employed person (sole trader) or as a partner, or whether the business is separately taxed as a limited company. Sole traders pay on the annual net profits of the business which are regarded for tax purposes as their gross income. Note that pre-tax net profits are gross income. They become net income after tax has been deducted. The whole of the net profits will be taxed and not just the amount that is withdrawn for private and personal use.

The sole trader's own personal allowances will be claimed in the normal way when making the tax return to the Inland Revenue. It is important to remember that even though the whole of the profits are taxed as though they were the trader's personal income this should not be regarded as a licence to spend the entire profits on personal matters. No business can develop if it is starved of funds. A business cannot stand still for long and sooner or later a choice has to be made between advance or decline. Even merely to maintain existing standards will require some reinvestment by using a proportion of the profits just to keep the premises in good order, to replace ageing or out-dated equipment and introduce new methods and new materials. It may appear to be something of a contradiction to say that although in legal terms the sole trader and the business are one person in terms of financial liability it is nevertheless essential from the point of view of good management to see them as separate identities each with independent and competing claims on available profits.

Tax evasion and tax avoidance

It is always as well to be aware of the distinction between tax evasion and tax avoidance. Tax evasion means exactly what it says, which is deliberately to misrepresent trading figures in order to evade payment of tax which is legitimately due, and such actions are a criminal offence punishable by due process of law. On the other hand tax avoidance is common practice in businesses of all shapes and sizes and simply means avoiding unnecessary payment of tax by claiming all appropriate reliefs. This can sometimes be quite a complicated affair requiring an intimate knowledge of taxation law. There are tax experts who make a living advising on such matters but for the average sole trader it is more a question of making sure that all legitimate costs and expenses have been included in the final accounts and all personal reliefs have been claimed when preparing the tax return. If in doubt it is a relatively simple matter to seek the free advice of the local Tax Inspector.

Final accounts

All that now remains is to make brief comments on the relevant final accounts.

Trial balance

This is a list of all of the debit and credit balances extracted from the ledger accounts, including cash and bank balances from the cash book. The trial balance performs two main functions. It provides:

* a means of checking the arithmetical accuracy of the postings in the ledger;
* a complete list of ledger balances from which to prepare the trading account, the profit and loss account, and the balance sheet.

As with the balance sheet the trial balance does not actually form part of the double-entry system.

Trading account

The first purpose of the trading account is to discover the gross profit for the trading period under review, not exclusively for the amount in itself but also to assist in knowing the ratio of gross profit to revenue (turnover) and the value of the ratio for comparison with similar information from preceding business years.

Profit and loss account

The purpose of the profit and loss account is to take the gross profit and discover the net profit for the trading period under review by a process of deducting all legitimate business expenses. The ratio of net profit to revenue is of value in revealing the relationship between gross profit and net profit over the current and preceding business years.

Balance sheet

The purpose of the balance sheet is to present a true and correct view of the total financial position of the business at a given date. It is prepared from the balances of the accounts that remain open in the ledger after the preparation of the trading account and the profit and loss account. The Balance Sheet will also provide the current asset and current liability figures which can be used to determine the liquidity of the business at that time.

The purpose of this chapter has been to attempt to acquaint the owner/manager with most of the accounts and records which could and often should be used in a sole trader business. Clearly it is possible for a business to function satisfactorily with a necessary minimum of accounting strategies but since it is essential to know not only where you are now but also where you are going in the future it is better to err on the side of too much information rather than too little.

The volume and complexity of the trading will determine to a great extent how much time needs to be given over to bookkeeping but whatever that may be it is almost bound to be time well spent, even if only to be sure that you have got your finger on the financial pulse of your business. Last but by no means least, remember that complete and accurate accounts and records maintained throughout the trading year will save your accountant's time and your money when the final accounts come to be prepared.

14 Some aspects of law

Law is absolutely essential to regularize the functions of society and to protect the interests of the individual and the state. Most people would consider themselves to be law-abiding and yet the majority will commit at least minor breaches of the law on a number of occasions during their lifetime. This is not difficult to understand if we remember that practically everything we do is covered by law of one kind or another.

The law of our country comprises Common Law and Statute Law (Acts of Parliament). The most fundamental part of the law is Common Law which is a body of rules which have evolved out of the decisions of High Court judges in respect of disputes brought before them over many generations. However, the supreme power of law-making is vested in Parliament. Common Law can thus be overridden by Acts of Parliament which constitute Statute Law. The law consists then of the words of Acts of Parliament, or Regulations and Orders made thereunder; of byelaws made by Local Authorities and of Common Law rules developed in settling legal disputes.

The law can be divided broadly into two components, criminal law and civil law. Criminal law can be described as a code of conduct demanded from an individual by society as a whole. In business the word individual would equally include the sole trader, a partnership or a limited company. Proceedings under criminal law are normally initiated by the state itself or through the agency of some public official such as a Health and Safety Inspector or a police officer. Civil law is the law which governs the relationships between individuals and is enforceable only by the individual. The state generally has no active interest in transgression under civil law except where it also infringes the criminal code. Whereas criminal law seeks to punish the offence against it civil law seeks to compensate the injured party (the plaintiff) at the expense of the wrongdoer. The injured party therefore sues the defaulting party (the defendant) for one of the remedies available such as damages (compensation). It should be noted that the expression 'injured party' does not necessarily refer to physical injury. An injured party can simply suffer loss, unfair dismissal, discrimination and so on.

In this book, only those parts of business law and employment law which seem to have the greatest relevance to a hairdressing or beauty therapy business are discussed – in the simplest terms. Where it is considered the reader may wish to pursue a particular matter in greater depth appropriate book titles are given under the heading of Further Reading. Law is without doubt a fascinating subject and at least some of those who take up this suggestion may find themselves hooked for years to come.

It must be emphasized that while the primary purpose of the text which follows is to leave the employer and/or manager better informed with regard to their responsibilities it is always prudent to seek professional advice in any unusual situation.

The law of contract

Contracts are commonplace. All people are constantly entering into contracts of one kind or another during the daily course of their lives whether it is by travelling on a train or bus, buying or selling goods and services, or employing people or being employed. We tend to think of contracts as legal documents signed by the parties concerned and indeed some contracts are of this kind but the vast majority of daily contracts are either verbal or merely implied by our actions and the actions of others.

When a client requests an appointment for a permanent wave or a manicure and the receptionist books that appointment we have a contract whereby the client agrees to attend at a certain time on a particular day and to pay the price stated, while the management agrees to carry out that service at that time on that day, most of which is implied by the actions of requesting and booking the appointment. It is also implied that the work will be completed to the reasonable satisfaction of the client.

It is doubtful if a dissatisfied client would attempt to sue the employer except where negligence was involved and actual loss or injury was suffered. Nevertheless it is important not to make extravagant claims regarding the effectiveness or outcome of a given process which cannot be reasonably substantiated because, negligence apart, a dissatisfied client is bad for business and such situations should be avoided whenever possible.

It is not unusual for an appointment to fail to be kept and although in such a case the client is technically in breach of contract it would not pay the management to pursue the matter and so it is generally accepted as a normal business hazard.

Contracts between employers and employees

In essence a contract of employment is no different from any other contract although under current legislation it is constrained by a number of statutory provisions which at least seek to regulate some of the terms and conditions under which people work.

As with other contracts all that is actually required is a process of offer and acceptance, neither of which needs to be in writing provided the employee is ultimately given a statement of the main terms and conditions of employment. An exception can be found in the field of hairdressing in the case of an apprentice where the law insists there must be a formal deed of apprenticeship which is duly signed and witnessed.

There is no reason why a full written contract of employment, as opposed to a mere statement of terms and conditions, should not be generally applied and many employers actually prefer to do this to reduce the possibility of disputes at some later date. Nevertheless while in theory a formal contract of employment binds the parties to the written terms and conditions therein it is not always quite so simple a matter when changing circumstances are involved raising questions of what was implied or intended and what may now be regarded as possible or reasonable.

Apprenticeship contracts

The essential difference between an apprenticeship contract and a normal contract of employment is that one of the parties to the contract (the apprentice) is almost invariably under age and in law is regarded as an infant or minor.

In law both contracts of service and contracts of apprenticeship are binding on an infant only when they can stand up to the test that the contract as a whole is beneficial to the infant. An apprenticeship contract implies service on the part of the apprentice and teaching on the part of the master (employer). Therefore, beneficial in this context implies that at the end of the term the apprentice should be capable of earning a living in the designated craft or industry. It would be reasonable to suppose that just as failure to give satisfactory service on the part of the apprentice could be regarded as a breach of contract so a failure on the part of the master to teach the apprentice, or cause the apprentice to be taught, might also be regarded as a breach of contract.

An apprenticeship contract must be in writing and signed under witness by the parties thereto, which generally consist of the master, the apprentice and a parent or guardian.

The normal conditions applicable to contracts of employment as required by the current legislation must either be included in the contract of apprenticeship or in a separate written statement.

An apprenticeship contract is a fixed term contract and while it is not subject to specific conditions of notice the date of termination must be stated. When employment continues after the date of termination of the apprenticeship a new contract of employment or a statement of employment containing all of the terms and conditions relevant to the employee's new status must be provided. In these circumstances the period of apprenticeship will count as part of continuous employment.

Employment protection legislation

From the point of view of business one of the most significant aspects of statute law which has received much attention in the last two or three decades has been concerned with protecting the interests of employees. Even a trader with only one employee, other than members of the family, must comply with the relevant provisions of the various Acts and associated legislation.

Written statement of employment

Under normal circumstances each employee must receive a written statement of the terms and conditions of employment within thirteen weeks of the starting date. At the present time such a statement should contain at least the following information:

* name of employer and employee;
* date of commencement of employment (if earlier employment is to count as part of the continuous period of employment this must be stated and the earlier date specified);
* hours of work;

* rate of pay, overtime, commission and/or bonuses together with dates payment is to be made;
* pension rights if applicable;
* entitlement to holiday, holiday pay and sick pay;
* disciplinary and safety rules;
* length of notice of termination of employment.

At the present time a person continuously employed for a period of 4 weeks is entitled to not less than 1 week's notice and a person continuously employed for between 2 and 12 years must receive 1 week's notice for each year of continuous service. Continuous employment for over 12 years requires not less than 12 weeks notice. On the other hand the employer is only entitled to 1 week's notice from an employee who has been employed for 4 or more weeks. Although the above periods of notice cannot be shortened even by agreement, payment of wages may be offered to the employee in lieu of notice.

Contract of employment

A contract of employment differs from a statement of employment in that it implies an individual contract resulting from negotiation and formal agreement of its terms by the parties thereto. However, a contract of employment will generally contain much the same information as a statement unless there are specific conditions applicable to the employing organization, the workforce, or the nature of the work.

Although a number of time-honoured implied terms of employment have been handed down through Common Law the statement of employment and the contract of employment both regularize the matter and impose a known legal framework at the outset. Clearly terms and conditions of employment and their implementation are no longer entirely at the discretion of the employer and while all is still not perfect most employees have quite considerable protection which their forebears did not enjoy.

Wages

Wages are in general either offered or negotiated and where a workforce is adequately represented by a strong trade union, wage agreements and sometimes terms and conditions of employment are the subject of collective bargaining. Where,

however, the employees have no effective union represen-
tation it is the current policy to operate Wages Councils to
represent the interests, albeit minimum interests, of the
workers.

Even so, it is still up to the individual employer and market
forces to determine how much is offered over and above the
legal minimum. Clearly, a great deal would depend on the
practical skill, productive ability and personality of each employee and their real value to the business in terms of revenue
generated.

Owners and/or managers of hairdressing or beauty therapy
businesses would do well to bear in mind that inadequately
paid members of staff are hardly likely to be as loyal and
productive as those who receive satisfactory financial rewards
for their work.

Itemized pay statement

An itemized pay statement must be provided with each
payment of wages and must give at least the following information:

* full details of the gross wage including overtime, commission and/or bonus payments;
* any fixed and/or variable deductions from that gross wage;
* the final net wage.

Any variable deductions must be separately itemized and
explained but in the case of fixed deductions the employer may
simply issue to the employee, at least every 12 months, a
standing statement of the amount of the deductions and the
intervals between them and then simply refer in the itemized
pay statement to the full total of the fixed deductions.

It must be understood that the only deductions which can at
present legally be made without prior agreement are Income
Tax (PAYE) and National Insurance contributions.

Equality at work

There has always been discrimination of one kind or another
in employment for reasons other than levels of ability and
qualification and a number of statutes have been enacted in
recent years in an attempt to remove unreasonable inequality
in the workplace.

Racial discrimination

Racial discrimination in this country has gained considerable attention largely as a post-war phenomenon highlighted by the increased numbers of people from other parts of the world who have been allowed to enter and make their homes here. The Race Relations Act of 1976 makes it unlawful for an employer to discriminate against an employee or potential employee simply on grounds of race. This somewhat simplified statement summarizes very briefly the general principle behind which are quite complex provisions.

Racial discrimination can be direct, indirect, or by way of victimization and this alone suggests that the nature of the offence will depend much upon the manner and circumstances in which it occurs.

Sex discrimination

The war against sex discrimination began with the Equal Pay Act of 1970, which did not come into force until 1975, together with the Sex Discrimination Act of 1975. The two Acts deal primarily with different aspects of discrimination, the 1970 Act dealing with all those aspects of employment covered in the contract of employment itself and the 1975 Act with all other areas of employment.

The initial concept is that it is unlawful for an employer to discriminate against an employee or potential employee on what may be loosely described as grounds of sex.

Equal pay

Under the Equal Pay Act it is required that every contract of employment of a woman must be deemed in law to contain an equality clause which in effect gives every woman two guarantees which are in essence:

* that where she is employed upon similar work to a man in the same employment then the terms of the woman's contract shall be no less favourable to her than the man's is to him and shall include all benefits which exist under the main contract;
* where it can be shown that a woman is employed in work rated as equivalent to that of a man in the same employment then the woman's contract in terms of pay shall be no less favourable to her than the man's is to him. *In other words men and women shall receive equal pay for equal work.*

Vacancies

When advertising vacancies and interviewing candidates it is important to remember that jobs must be open to all races and both sexes. A business that employs fewer than six people is normally exempt from sex discrimination provisions but not from those of race.

Maternity rights

An obvious indirect way in which a woman may be discriminated against is to treat her less favourably than other employees because she is pregnant.

The Employment Act of 1980 gives the pregnant employee four rights, namely:

* the right to time off for antenatal visits;
* the right not to be dismissed on grounds of pregnancy alone;
* the right to Statutory Maternity Pay (SMP);
* the right to return to work following her confinement.

Subject to the provision of a doctor's documentary confirmation the employer is bound to allow reasonable time off with pay for the purpose of antenatal visits.

Under normal circumstances a woman may not be dismissed on grounds of pregnancy and in such an event may claim against the employer for unfair dismissal.

Subject to continuous employment requirements and correctly notifying the employer at least 21 days before the intended date of leaving, the pregnant employee is entitled to SMP equal to 9/10ths or 90 per cent of normal pay for a period of six weeks absence and up to a further 12 weeks pay at a lower rate (as notified from time to time by the DHSS). Payments of SMP may be recovered by the employer by deduction from national insurance contributions.

Subject to continuous employment requirements and to the employee giving to the employer 21 days notice before leaving or as soon after as reasonably possible of her intention to return to work the employer is bound to keep her job open for her.

The term continuous employment currently requires the employee to have been continuously employed by the same employer for a minimum of 16 hours per week for two years or for five years where the employee has worked for less than 16 hours but not less than 8.

Maternity legislation is somewhat complex and the reader is advised to seek professional advice when in any doubt.

Discrimination in general

Quite obviously whether it is a question of sex, race, or for that matter disability, a person must be capable of filling a post and continuing to perform their duties satisfactorily.

Discrimination can be either direct or indirect. For example, direct discrimination means discriminating against a woman simply because she is a woman, whereas indirect discrimination would mean imposing unjustifiable conditions which a woman would be less able to meet than a man.

Clearly there are some occupations and some types of work which for very personal reasons could be regarded as unsuitable for either men or women but bearing in mind the increasing freedom implied in changing social attitudes it is not inconceivable that even these remaining reservations may also disappear in the course of time.

Finally it must be remembered that women are not the only victims of sex discrimination and although the number of instances may be fewer it is perfectly possible for men also to be discriminated against.

Terminating employment

At Common Law a contract of employment can come to an end in any one of four main ways:

* by the giving of notice;
* by expiry of a fixed term;
* by summary dismissal;
* by automatic termination.

In principle, employment may be terminated by either party giving the correct amount of notice contained in the contract but in practice it is not quite as simple as that. While the contract itself might specify a given period of notice this could be at variance with the requirements of current legislation, which are that the employer must give:

* at least one week's notice after four weeks of employment;
* two week's notice after two years of employment;
* a further week's notice for every additional year of employment up to a maximum of twelve.

The employee is required to give only one week's notice regardless of the length of employment.

The parties may agree longer periods of notice on either side but shorter periods than those required by the Act will be void.

The employee must receive normal pay during the period of notice or may consent to pay in lieu of notice but cannot be legally compelled to do so.

The failure of either party to give the minimum statutory period of notice or any extended period of notice agreed in the contract, or to pay wages that are due will enable the aggrieved party to sue.

The expiry of a fixed term contract without renewal can have complications in respect of unfair dismissal or redundancy, except in the case of an apprenticeship contract.

Summary dismissal is a situation in which the employee is dismissed without notice or payment in lieu of notice. This can only be justified in cases of extreme misdemeanour on the part of the employee and in other circumstances could constitute unfair dismissal.

Automatic termination can occur when a contract becomes frustrated in that it is no longer possible to continue because of some intervening event such as imprisonment of the employee, long-term illness or death of the employee.

Under current legislation the employer is required to furnish a dismissed employee with a written statement, within 14 days of demand, giving particulars of the reason for dismissal, provided the employee has been at least 26 weeks in continuous employment.

In certain circumstances dismissal could be wrongful under Common Law or unfair under the relevant statute.

Unfair dismissal

In essence under the requirements of the Employment Acts the majority of employees have the right not to be unfairly dismissed but in order to qualify for this right the employee must have been in continuous employment by the same employer for a minimum of 16 hours per week for a minimum period of one year where there are more than twenty in staff or two years where there are less than twenty in staff.

The matter is once again not quite as simple as that and there are a number of circumstances which can vary this requirement. The reader is advised to seek professional advice in any situation where the possibility of a claim for unfair dismissal could arise.

It would perhaps be easier to determine what constitutes fair dismissal rather than unfair dismissal. No one would expect an employer to put up with a worker who was obviously incompetent, prone to continuous absence for reasons of chronic ill-health, or guilty of persistent misconduct.

At one time an employee was required to prove unfair treatment but now the tables are turned and the onus of proof is entirely upon the employer to show that the employee was in fact fairly dismissed.

In order to justify dismissal as fair the employer must satisfy three tests, which are to:

* identify the reason for dismissal;
* show that the reason was fair;
* show that action towards the employee was reasonable.

Clearly there are a number of situations which could result in fair dismissal and others that might lead to dismissal which could be shown to be unfair. In every case brought the rightness or wrongness of the matter is determined through the deliberations of the appropriate Tribunal and anyone involved in such a situation would be well advised to take professional advice. Under almost any circumstances it would be unwise for management to dismiss an employee in the heat of the moment. An employee should be dismissed only after all of the facts have been given due consideration and then strictly in accordance with the requirements of employment law which includes the giving of fair warnings prior to the act of dismissal.

Negligence and the law of torts

A tort is a breach of a civil duty imposed by Common Law. A tort is a civil wrong which may be redressed by an action for damages.

A tort which is of particular significance to the practising hairdresser or beauty therapist is the tort of negligence. There have been many definitions of negligence but one which fits the bill quite well is 'an unreasonable disregard of the foreseeable likelihood of harm or unreasonable failure to foresee the possibility of harm'. Clearly negligence can result both from acts of commission and acts of omission, that is to say, something we did that we should not have done or something we should have done but did not do. It should not be too difficult for those who work in a hairdressing or beauty therapy salon to think of a number of things which could fit either description.

Vicarious liability

Common Law states that 'a master is liable for the torts that his servants commit in the course of their employment'. In the case of a hairdressing or beauty therapy salon the employer is the master and the employees the servants. Therefore in general terms if an employee causes injury to a client the employer is responsible. What is meant by the expression 'in the course of their employment' is not easily defined but in general it covers all normal activities authorized by the employer.

Consent

Some managers appear to be under the impression that if the client gives written consent to a process being carried out and does so in full awareness of any danger involved no action can be taken in the event of a mishap. But there is still the question of negligence and since the client is entitled to believe the operative to be reasonably competent to carry out the process and exercise all due care then if negligence can be proven the consent is not worth the paper it is written on.

There are three main ingredients to proof of negligence. The plaintiff (the client) is required to show that:

* the defendant (the operative) owed a duty of care;
* the defendant was in breach of that duty;
* loss or injury resulted from that breach.

In reality, since the employer can be held responsible for the acts of employees in the course of their employment and because the employer is most likely to have access to the means to meet any claim for damages the action is likely to be against the employer rather than the employee, in which case the employer would be the defendant.

Duty of care

Duty of care is a Common Law requirement and there is no statute which demands a similar overall duty. In the world of business, duty of care means, in general terms, an obligation to act towards customers or clients in a manner which will reasonably protect them against foreseeable loss or injury. This duty is not confined to processes carried out on the person as in the case of hairdressing or beauty therapy but includes the reasonable fitness of the premises and their contents for the purposes for which they are provided and the general safety and well-being of all those who are invited to enter thereon.

Employer's liability

A duty of care applies equally between employer and employee and in accordance with Common Law a master (employer) owes his servant (employee) a duty to ensure that reasonable care is taken to provide:

* competent fellow servants (workers);
* safe and adequate equipment;
* safe systems of work;
* a safe place of work and access thereto.

Various statutes impose a number of other duties on employers, the most comprehensive of which is the Health and Safety at Work Act of 1974.

It is not simply the employer who is responsible for the safety of the workplace. All employees are under a duty while at work to take reasonable care for their own safety and the safety of anyone else who may be affected by their acts or omissions at work and to cooperate with the employer in the performance of any duty of safety imposed by virtue of the Act.

Contributory negligence. Any employee who fails to take reasonable care for their own safety and is subsequently injured may be guilty of contributory negligence which means that the employee contributed to the circumstances which resulted in the injury sustained. This could proportionately reduce the amount of any compensation which might be awarded.

Employer's indemnity. An employer who has been made liable for an employee's negligence may:

* claim a contribution from the employee under the Civil Liability (Contribution) Act of 1978; or
* sue the employee for damages for breach of an implied term of the contract of employment provided the employer is free from blame.

The employer also has a duty to ensure that employees are competent to carry out the tasks assigned to them and will exercise due care in so doing. It may be difficult, therefore, other than in exceptional circumstances to show that the employer was entirely free from blame.

Clearly it is safer for management to maintain the strictest surveillance over all work done, insist on every reasonable precaution being taken and at no time allow inexperienced members of staff to undertake any hazardous tasks on their own initiative.

Insurance

Employers are required by the Employer's Liability (Compulsory Insurance) Act of 1969 to maintain an approved insurance policy with authorized insurers so as to meet the eventuality of a claim in respect of injury or disease arising out of and in the course of employment.

Health and Safety at Work Act 1974

While Common Law requires the employer to take reasonable care for the safety of employees and anyone else who may be injured by careless behaviour, under Common Law the penalty for default comes after the event. In practice the aim is not so much to prevent accidents but to establish who is liable. A number of statutes have been enacted with the aim of putting pressure on the employer to provide an environment in which accidents are less likely to occur and the latest and most comprehensive of these is the Health and Safety at Work Act of 1974. Under these regulations all employers are under the same safety code, and proof of injury is no longer required before action can be taken against default. Mere failure to provide or apply statutory safeguards is an offence in itself and can result in legal action against the employer.

Section 2 of the Act states that it shall be the duty of every employer to ensure so far as is reasonably practicable the health and safety at work of employees. While this appears similar to the Common Law duty of care the essential difference is that while Common Law gives the employee the right to sue for damages in the event of actually being injured, under the 1974 Act the employer is liable to prosecution for breach regardless of whether or not an accident has resulted.

Section 2 also requires every employer with five or more workers to prepare and issue, and revise whenever necessary, a written statement of general safety policy with regard to the health and safety of employees and the arrangements for making the policy effective. This statement must be brought to the notice of all employees.

Employers' duties owed to other parties

Section 3 of the Act also imposes a duty on every employer (even every self-employed person engaged in business activity) to conduct their operations in such a way as to ensure so far as is reasonably practicable that other persons are not thereby exposed to risks to their health and safety.

Duties owed by employees

Section 7 of the Act also requires employees to take reasonable care while at work for their own safety and that of anyone else who may be affected by their acts or omissions and to cooperate with the employer in any duty of safety imposed on the latter by virtue of the Act.

Enforcement of the provisions of the Health and Safety at Work Act. The enforcement of the 1974 Act is the ultimate responsibility of the Health and Safety Executive who appoint inspectors under the Act to enforce its provisions. But in the case of business premises designated primarily as offices or shops – which includes hairdressing and beauty therapy salons – enforcement remains in the hands of the local authority, the original enforcers of the Offices, Shops and Railway Premises Act of 1963. The 1963 Act has survived the passing of the 1974 Act and its provisions still provide the main detailed rules of safety in premises covered by it, subject to the overall duties of safety laid down by the 1974 Act.

Fire precautions

The Fire Precautions Act of 1971 requires that all occupiers of business premises in which more than twenty persons are employed (ten where they are employed above ground level) shall obtain a fire certificate from the local fire authority. Even those premises which do not require such a fire certificate must comply with Regulations issued in 1976 under which there must be clear markings on fire exit doors, the provision of fire fighting equipment and an easy means of escape from rooms in which people are employed.

Defective equipment

The Employers' Liability (Defective Equipment) Act of 1969 makes the employer liable should an employee sustain personal injury in the course of employment in consequence of a defect in equipment provided by the employer for the purpose of the employer's business. Clearly it is sound policy for management in hairdressing and beauty therapy salons to ensure that all electrical equipment is checked at regular intervals by a qualified person.

Business premises and their usage

It is important to appreciate that occupiers of business premises cannot do exactly as they like. As the majority of business premises are much more likely to be leased rather than owned, the tenancy will be subject to terms and conditions imposed by the landlord or lessor. There will also be regulations as to use determined by the local authority. Even when the occupier owns the property it will still be subject to local byelaws under the Town and Country Planning Acts and associated legislation which will not only limit its use but also place planning restrictions on any substantial alterations which may be envisaged.

The local authority is also charged under the Public Health Act of 1936 with a duty to maintain standards of public health and all business premises are likely to be subject to inspection on that count alone from time to time.

Occupier's liability

At Common Law an occupier of business premises owes a legal duty to those who enter upon the premises to ensure that they are reasonably safe for them to do so and the Occupier's Liability Act of 1957 repeats this in statutory form stating basically that the occupier owes a common duty of care to all visitors who enter upon the premises.

Consumer protection

The Trade Descriptions Act of 1968 is an early example of consumer protection legislation. Briefly under Section 1 of the Act (offences in relation to goods) and under Section 14 (offences in relation to services) it is a criminal offence for any person in the course of any trade or business to apply a description to any goods or services offered or supplied which is false to a material degree. A false trade description can take almost any form, even simple appearances. Thus the picture on the packet of an item for sale could be regarded as a description of what is inside the packet. This condition applies equally to services in any form of publicity or advertising.

Under Section 14 (services) the description or statement must have been made knowingly and recklessly without caring whether it was true or false. If the trader honestly believed it to be true it is likely no offence will have been committed. However, since it would be necessary to prove honest belief it is always wiser to avoid statements which could possibly be regarded as materially false. It is, of course, to be hoped that responsible management would not wish to build a business on deliberate falsehoods.

The Act also requires, under Section 11, that reduced price offers should be genuine and to qualify as a genuine reduction the goods or services must have been on offer at a higher price for a period of at least twenty-eight days in the previous six months.

Tax law

It is not proposed to comment on tax law because the position is perfectly clear in that we are all required to pay, as appropriate, Value Added Tax, Income Tax and National Insurance contributions; also rates which are a kind of local tax. Anyone who fails to meet their liabilities in these respects may find themselves subject to due process of law.

Queries regarding any of these should be addressed to:

* the local Tax Office on matters of Income Tax;
* the local Customs and Excise Office on matters of Value Added Tax;
* the local Department of Health and Social Security on matters of National Insurance contributions;
* the rates department of the Local Authority on matters of rates.

Information appropriate to accounting for PAYE, National Insurance contributions, VAT and Schedule D Income Tax will be found in the concluding pages of the chapter on Keeping the Books.

While the statutory references contained in this chapter are applicable at the time of writing it is reasonable to suppose that some new and/or revised legislation in respect of business and/or employment law may appear subsequent to publication. Any such changes may be verified by enquiry addressed to the appropriate government department.

Relevant Acts

Legislation affecting business activities is extensive and much of it would be only of marginal interest to the sole trader operating on a modest scale. Below, however, are some statutory references which may prove to be of interest to the reader:

* Contracts of Employment Act 1972;
* Consumer Credit Act 1974;
* Defective Premises Act 1972;
* Employers' Liability (Compulsory Insurance) Act 1969;
* Employers' Liability (Defective Equipment) Act 1969;
* Equal Pay Act 1970;
* Employment Protection (Consolidation) Act 1978;
* Employment Acts 1980 and 1982;
* Fire Precautions Act 1971 and Fire Regulations Act 1976;
* Fair Trading Act 1973;
* Health and Safety at Work Act 1974;
* Landlord and Tenant Acts 1927 and 1954;
* Offices, Shops and Railway Premises Act 1963;
* Occupiers' Liability Acts 1957 and 1984;
* Race Relations Act 1976;
* Shops Act 1950;
* Sale of Goods (Implied Terms) Act 1973;
* Sex Discrimination Act 1975;
* Sale of Goods Act 1979;
* Supply of Goods and Services Act 1982;
* Trade Descriptions Acts 1968–72;
* Town and Country Planning Act 1971 and specific legislation relating to certain trades referred to therein.
* Legislation referring to the requirements of the Inland Revenue, Customs and Excise, Department of Health and Social Security.

Further reading

Two useful books provide more detailed information on accounts and business law for the small trader:

* *Mastering the Principles of Accounts*, J. Randall Stott, 1982, published by Macmillan Education Ltd, Houndmills, Basingstoke, Hampshire RG21 2XS.

* *Law for the Small Business*, Patricia Clayton, 1985, published by Kogan Page Ltd, 120 Pentonville Road, London N1 9JN.

Some useful official publications can be obtained free of charge from your local Tax Office and/or Department of Health and Social Security (DHSS):

	Ref. No.
* Thinking of working for yourself?	IR57
* Starting in business	IR28
* Thinking of taking someone on?	IR53
* Tax – employed or self-employed?	IR56
* Employer's guide to PAYE	P7
* National Insurance guide for the self-employed	NI41
* Employer's guide to National Insurance contributions	NP15
* Class 4 National Insurance contributions	NP18
* Memorandum on the computation of profits for Class 4 National Insurance contributions	IR24
* Capital allowances on machinery or plant	CA1

Obtainable from your local office of HM Customs and Excise:

	Ref. No.
* Should I be registered for VAT?	700/1
* The ins and outs of VAT	700/15
* Filling in your VAT return	700/12
* Keeping records and accounts (VAT)	700/21

* Value Added Tax – the VAT guide   700
* Value Added Tax – retail schemes   727
* VAT liability law   701/39A

Obtainable from Small Firms Division of the Department of Trade and Industry:

* Starting your own business – the practical steps
* Running your own business – planning for success
* Employing people
* Elements of book-keeping
* Management accounting

Obtainable from the Advisory Conciliation and Arbitration Service (ACAS):

* Employing people

City and Guilds of London Institute Examinations

This book which is a companion volume to the author's well known *Hairdressing in Theory and Practice* will prove to be of considerable relevance and interest to candidates preparing for any of the following examinations:

300   HAIRDRESSING

300   ADVANCED STUDIES IN HAIRDRESSING

304   BEAUTY THERAPY

306   SALON MANAGEMENT

Appropriate syllabuses together with conditions of entry can be obtained from the:

Sales Section,
City and Guilds of London Institute,
76 Portland Place,
London,
W1N 4AA.

Telephone 01-580 3050

Index